FLORIDA INT

MW00880480

Dear Panther,

Welcome to the 2019-2020 academic year at FIU! This is an exciting time to begin your university education – a time for personal advancement and exploration. On behalf of FIU, I would like to introduce you to your first assignment as a college student.

The Common Reading Program unites our first-year students through a shared intellectual experience. Each year, a book is chosen with the hope of igniting meaningful discussions. You are expected to read this book before the first day of classes, and over the course of the semester, you will discuss the book with your classmates and engage in experiential opportunities relative to the themes in the book.

As you continue on your academic career and participate in the numerous opportunities inside and outside of the classroom, we hope Martin's story will inspire you to create a life of meaning and purpose. Your journey begins with successfully completing your degree at FIU within four years and continues with a meaningful career after graduation.

We look forward to the new school year and many exciting opportunities for academic enrichment and community engagement. Best wishes for a successful and productive year!

Sincerely,

Valerie J. Johnsen
Associate Provost for Academic and Career Success

DETERMINED

A Memoir

ONE BOY'S
HOLOCAUST
SURVIVAL
STORY

MARTIN BARANEK
with LISA B. CICERO

ACKNOWLEDGMENTS

Martin Baranek

I want to thank my wife of 64 years, Betty Baranek. She has been a wonderful wife, mother, grandmother and friend to so many. She has stood by me all these years, which has not always been easy and she has supported me in my efforts to return to Poland and Israel again and again as I share my story with those who have accompanied me on the March of the Living.

I want to thank my children, the late Morry, his wife Arlene, and their children Reide, Palmer, and Brett, my son Mark and his wife, Nava, my son Lenny and his wife, Ita, and their children, Hayley, Jamie and Sam, and my daughter, Marlene, and her children, Brandon, Jenna, and Cole.

I want to thank Lisa Cicero from the bottom of my heart for being there for me these last several years, for the Ciceros being part of our Miami family, and for taking on this project. If it weren't for Lisa's persistence this book would not have been possible. I was constantly amazed at the historical information she was able to find out about my family, my town, and me through her research. Thank you for helping me to preserve my story for my family, and for future generations.

ACKNOWLEDGMENTS

Lisa B. Cicero

I WANT TO thank Marty Baranek for his willingness to work with me on this project and for trusting me with his remarkable story. In 2005 I participated in the March of the Living commemorating the 60th anniversary of the end of the war. Most evenings after long and emotionally draining days, Marty, and fellow survivor, Leo Martin, would tell me of their very different experiences during the Holocaust. Marty could stand in front of a group in the barracks at Auschwitz-Birkenau and tell his life story, but he had never written any of it down. He agreed to memorialize it in writing for the sake of his family, and the sake of history. Over time, the project grew into this book that details one boy's survival story.

I also want to thank the saintly Betty Baranek who has supported this project from the beginning and who herself is a survivor having spent the war years in Siberia, and in a DP camp.

Thank you also to Mark and Nava Baranek. Mark was the Holocaust educator on each of the March of the Living trips I attended. Thank you also to Lenny and Ita Baranek, and their children, Hayley, Jamie and Sam, Marlene Baranek, and her children, Brandon, Jenna, and Cole, and Reide, Palmer, and Brett, children of the late Morry Baranek and Arlene Baranek for their willingness to share Marty with all the marchers who have traveled to Poland and Israel with him.

Thank you to the early readers of the manuscript for their very helpful edits, comments, and suggestions including J.R. Rosskamp McDowell, Betsy Mateu, Stephanie Rosen (my roommate on the 2011 March of the Living), Lisa Rosen, Bonnie Berman, and Sonia Taitz. The daughter of Holocaust survivors, Sonia's own memoir, The Watchmaker's Daughter, inspired me to help Marty with his book and gave me insight in to the effects of the Holocaust on the next generation. A big thank you to Robin Rosenbaum Andras for her review of the manuscript and all things graphic and design related, along with Christa Williams for the design of the family tree and map of Marty's journey, and to the entire team at Damonza for cover design and interior design layout.

Thank you also to Christopher R. Browning, Frank Porter Graham Professor of History Emeritus, University of North Carolina at Chapel Hill, and author of Remembering Survival, a book he was compelled to write after researching the trial of Walther Becker, the head of the German police in charge of Marty's town. Despite the testimony of 60 eyewitnesses, the trial ended in an acquittal. Browning interviewed numerous survivors from Marty's town, including Marty. Browning's comments greatly improved the manuscript and I am indebted to him for his keen historical knowledge.

I want to thank my editor Leonard Nash for his encouragement, praise, and careful review of the manuscript and for the many improvements he made to it. Leonard is the Florida Book Award Silver Medal recipient for his debut collection, You Can't Get There from Here and Other Stories.

Thank you to my parents, Neil and Sandra Malamud, for sharing in the March of the Living with me in 2011 and 2013. Thank you to my children, Alexandra, Jordan, and Marina for their support and their understanding as to why this project, although time-consuming, is so important. Their relationship with Marty and Betty is a blessing, and I am thankful that they see Marty as their hero.

DEDICATION

This book, which is based upon my memory and my own personal experience, is dedicated to my parents and my brother Chaskel and to all the other victims of the Holocaust. May their memory be for a blessing, and may the world never forget the terrible lessons of this tragedy. Any historical inaccuracies are unintended. This book is based solely upon my memory of events that happened to my family, my town and to me.

A Note about spelling throughout the book: Most of the names contained in the book utilize the original Yiddish spellings. Upon arrival in Israel or North America many eastern Europeans changed the spelling of their names to something more Hebrew or English sounding. In some cases, individuals adopted an entirely new name. At times, the variation of spellings or the adoption of new names altogether created delays and confusion in helping survivors reunite with family members or friends.

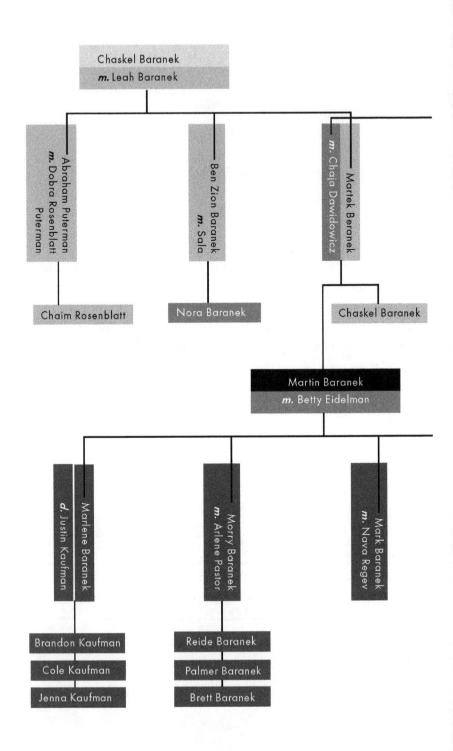

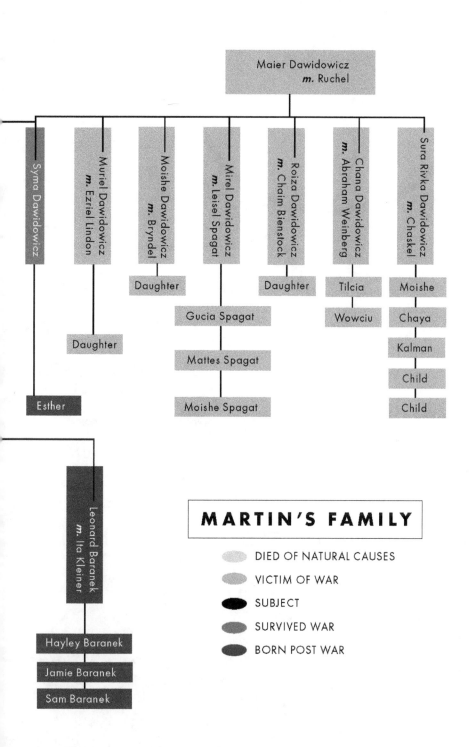

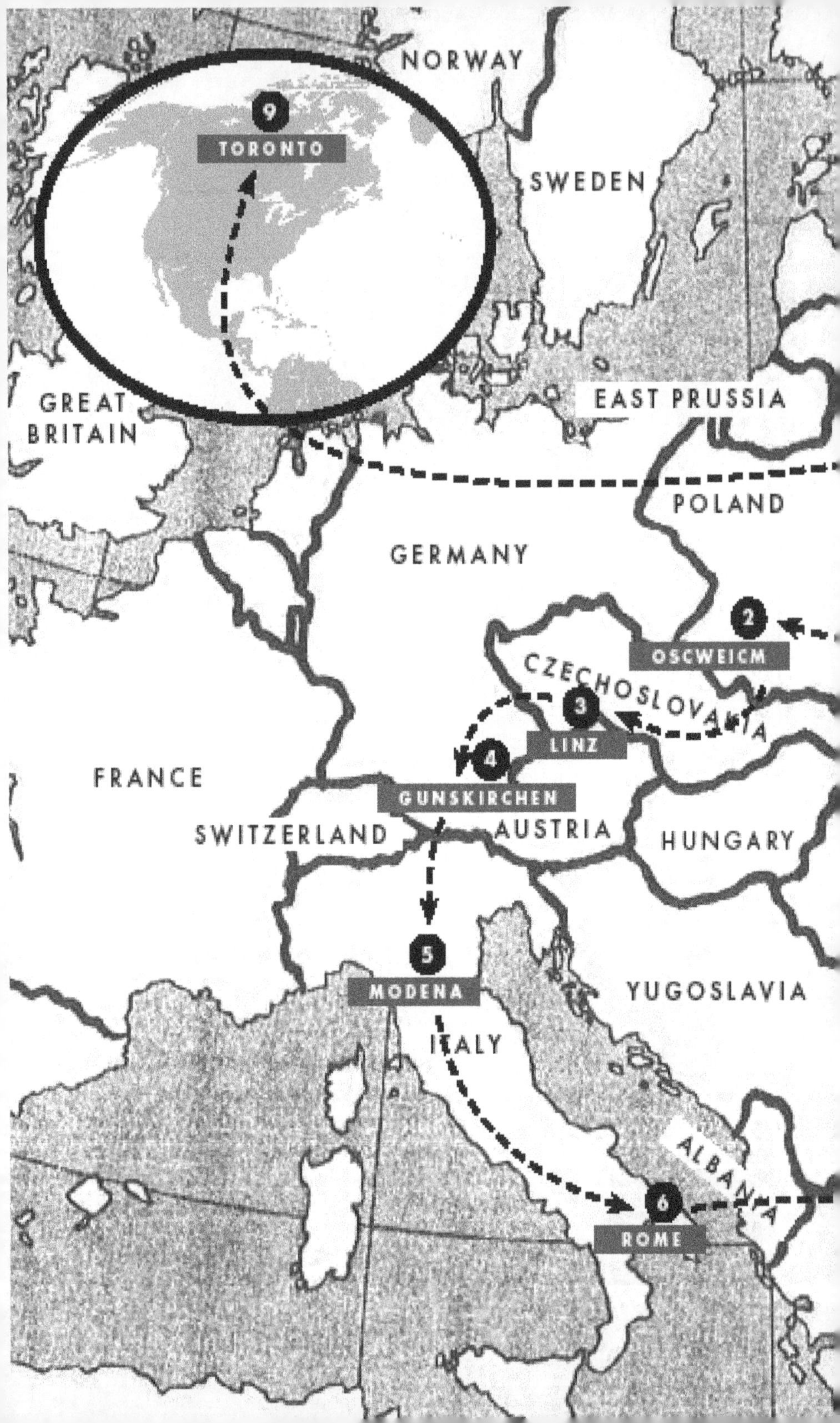

NORWAY

SWEDEN

EAST PRUSSIA

POLAND

GERMANY

GREAT
BRITAIN

TORONTO

9

2

OSCWEICM

CZECHOSLOVAKIA

3

LINZ

4

GUNSKIRCHEN

AUSTRIA

HUNGARY

FRANCE

SWITZERLAND

5

MODENA

ITALY

YUGOSLAVIA

6

ROME

ALBANIA

CONTENTS

PREFACE

Lisa B. Cicero

THIS IS THE story of the "Miracle Kid," the nickname given to Martin Baranek by his concentration camp brethren.

I am standing beside Martin in the town square of his former hometown of Wierzbnik, Poland. A taxi driver approaches and begins speaking to Martin in Polish. I can hear the anguish in the man's voice as he says to Martin, "I remember October 27, 1942. I was too young to do anything. I was just a child." He asks Martin what has become of his former classmates and neighbors. Martin tells him of the few who survived the war, but mostly of those who did not. The man has a helpless expression frozen in time on his aging face.

Martin is a regular participant in the March of the Living, an annual pilgrimage to Auschwitz-Birkenau on *Yom Hashoah*, Holocaust Remembrance Day. The purpose of the March is to educate students and adults, Jewish and non-Jewish alike, about the horrors of the Holocaust. Martin retells his life story while standing in the barracks in Birkenau. I convince him that his story must be memorialized for future generations, and he agrees to meet with me to document his experiences. He talks about life in Poland, and his struggle to recuperate in the war's aftermath. We travel together to Poland, Austria, and Israel on three separate occasions, visiting his hometown and the camps where he was a prisoner.

Martin's story is compelling because he experiences a ghetto, a labor camp, a concentration camp, and a death camp. By the age of 15, he also experiences a death march – and finally, liberation. Martin Baranek is the embodiment of the 20th century Eastern European Jewish experience.

Many wonder how and why one person survives the Holocaust while another does not, and whether place of birth or other circumstances play a part. Is it fate? Luck? Destiny? The answer is unknowable. For Martin, it may be his insuppressible spirit, or perhaps a series of miracles linked together that allowed him, one of the few from his family, to survive.

"For the dead and the living, we must bear witness."

—Elie Wiesel

INTRODUCTION

Martin Baranek

GOD TESTED ME. Like Job, he put stumbling blocks before me, and even though I survived, I no longer believe in God. How can I believe in a God who took my little brother, and a million and a half other children, children whose only crime was that they were born Jewish? How can I believe in a God when I was beaten, starved, and tormented without justification? I witnessed death and was surrounded by death. I cheated death – not once, but at least twice. Fear was my constant companion, like a shadow that followed me, but it did not extinguish even in the dark. I live each moment, despite the fear. I fear not what awaits me after this life, for I have survived indescribable misery and torment. Hell is living with the memory of what I have seen. Perhaps when it is my time, the movie reel that plays again and again in my mind will finally pause, and I will be able to sleep in peace. Perhaps heaven is having no memory of pain.

I am a Holocaust survivor, but physical survival is only one aspect of living through this tragedy. I lost everything – my childhood, my family, my dignity, my possessions, my security, and my belief in God. I was driven to make something of my life, to overcome obstacles, to learn new languages, to adapt to new cultures, and to create a new family. I did not want to remain forever "in the camps" psychologically, never to return to normalcy. No one survived the

Holocaust normal. After liberation, many organizations helped feed, clothe, and house us, but there were scarce resources to help survivors overcome tremendous emotional trauma, the torment of deprivation, and dehumanizing abuse and slavery. My generation was unlikely to seek out psychological counseling, or admit that post-traumatic stress disorder (PTSD) is real. Survivors coped the best they could, some better than others.

Few can say they are tested and know the depths of what they are made of – and what they can endure. Few can say that stripped of everything, they know their true essence, their true identity. Holocaust survivors know these things. I know these things.

After the war, I kept busy and moved forward with my life, not speaking about my past. Still, every night the movie reel played in my head. I still see the images, hear the screams, feel the pain as I attempt to sleep. I internalized much of my suffering, but I learned that one cannot outrun trauma. It has a way of manifesting itself and cannot be erased.

Each year at the Passover Seder, Jews around the world read the *Hagaddah,* the Jewish text that recounts the history of the Hebrew slaves in Egypt and their liberation from Pharaoh. During the service, we read that each of us is obliged to see ourselves as if we were personally freed from slavery, as if we, too, went forth from Egypt. For Holocaust survivors, this is something real. I don't have to imagine it. Survivors walk in the shoes of the Israelites, who transformed themselves from slaves of the Egyptian Pharaoh, to wanderers in the desert, before finally entering into the Promised Land. Upon our liberation from the Nazi Pharaohs, Holocaust survivors wandered in displaced persons camps (DP Camps), before arriving, mostly illegally, in far flung places around the globe. Many, including me, arrived in Palestine, our biblical homeland, the future State of Israel.

Many of my survivor friends never wanted to return to Europe after the war because it was a place of terrible memories and extreme loss. It remains the largest Jewish cemetery on earth, a cemetery without individual graves or headstones, but Alex Haley's *Roots* inspired me to return. In 1978, my wife Betty, and I traveled to Poland for the first time since the war. I did not mention the trip to my many survivor friends. "Why go back?" my friends would have asked. I had many reasons to revisit: to walk the streets of my childhood, to see the buildings and home of my past, to smell the flowers that adorned the gardens of my youth. I still struggle to make sense of it all, and I wanted desperately to feel close to the ones I once loved but have since lost. I wanted to honor and pay tribute to those dear to me who perished, and also to show respect to those who perished whom I never knew. I felt an overwhelming need to retrace my steps to remind myself that I did, in fact, survive. Returning serves as a reminder that nations, indeed entire civilizations, can, through open and dedicated involvement, or through passive inaction, be led down a path of evil. I do not fault anyone for failing to aid Jewish families at their own peril, but I will not forgive those who overtly took action to turn in Jews, to betray them, to commit atrocities.

For as long as I am able, I will make the pilgrimage each spring to remember and to bear witness. I believe it is a *mitzvah,* a good deed, to participate in The March of the Living. There is no better way to educate people than hearing survivor stories firsthand. Some survivors believe it is a *sin* to return to Poland, but I see it as an *opportunity* to teach what humans are capable of doing to their fellow human beings. It is important for people to hear it from someone with personal experience – not just to read about it in books, but to stand at the places where evil occurred and to try to ensure that genocide, of any kind and in any manner, does not happen again.

Christopher Browning, a history professor at the University of North Carolina who has written a number of books on the Holocaust, wanted to investigate the survival of Jews from the region of Poland known as Wierzbnik-Starachowice, where I was born and lived during my early youth. He contacted me for an interview for his book published in 2010 called *Remembering Survival: Inside a Nazi*

Slave-Labor Camp. The premise of the book, aside from Browning's theory of why a disproportionate number of Jews from Wierzbnik survived, is that individuals may remember the same events differently. According to Browning, a number of middle-class Jews with means procured work permits, and were thus protected in a factory where their skills were necessary for the war effort. Wierzbnik Jews with work permits were not relocated far from their homes and were able to access hidden money and valuables to sell or trade on the black market, and could make deals with factory guards or non-Jewish contacts outside the camp. Wierzbnik Jews were accustomed to a camp environment when the factories were eventually evacuated, and they were transported to concentration camps and death camps toward the latter part of the war.

Many survivors suffer in silence. Some details are just too painful or humiliating to impart to another human being. I have watched survivors break down in an attempt to just say out loud what happened to them, as if vocalizing it could create a physical wound. It is a burden to carry these heavy emotions and overwhelming memories. The world will never fully know all the atrocities the Nazi collaborators inflicted upon their victims. As much as what I share is terrible, there are occurrences far worse than what I am able to articulate. These will remain forever within me in a deep and hidden place.

To what do I attribute my survival? Was it *b'shert,* meant to be, or perhaps divine intervention? I have come to ascribe my survival to a series of large and small phenomena I call *miracles.*

From the private collection of Martin Baranek.

"Monsters exist, but they are too few in number to be truly dangerous. More dangerous are the common men, the functionaries ready to believe and to act without asking questions."

— Primo Levi

EARLY YEARS: MY CHILDHOOD IN THE SMALL TOWN OF WIERZBNIK, IN THE STARACHOWICE REGION, POLAND

"THE GERMANS HAVE invaded Poland. They are bombing Wierzbnik. Quickly, now, gather a few things. We will go to the countryside for a few days until things settle down. The coach is waiting for us downstairs." My father's tone was calm but suggested an urgency that he rarely revealed. We had been following the news from Germany, of course, and how things were deteriorating there, especially for the Jews, but we were relatively far away from the chaos of Germany. We were in southern Poland in the little town of Wierzbnik. I had always felt safe in our quaint town, insulated. Don't all nine-year-olds feel unassailable? Or perhaps my parents had sheltered us from big, grownup issues. I was raised with a sense of continuity. Generations of Jews, including my family, had lived and died in Poland, and I assumed as much for myself.

Wierzbnik, located in the Starachowice region, was founded in 1624 as a mining and metallurgical settlement. Until the early 1800s, the area was inhabited by the Cistercian monks of Wachock, who built a blast furnace in 1789. The Starzechowski family owned a forge built near the Kamienna River, a tributary of the Vistula River. As the population increased, weekly markets and annual fairs expanded. In the 1800s, the area continued to serve as a center of metallurgy, with iron foundries, ore mines, and a smelting furnace. The area was surrounded by dense forests and rolling hills, so lumberyards, sawmills, and a plywood factory were built in the vicinity. The late 1800s also saw the construction of a railway line linking the town to larger cities.

Life in Eastern Europe, where there has always been an undercurrent of anti-Semitism, has never been easy for Jews. The local population became wary of the growing Jewish population. Perhaps the majority felt threatened by the Jews' ingenuity, tenacity, and success, or perhaps their fears were just age-old xenophobia. The Jewish population was different, spoke a peculiar language, ate unfamiliar food, kept unknown traditions, such that in 1862, a decree was issued denying Jews the right to reside in Wierzbnik-Starachowice proper. Despite these early acts of anti-Semitism, the thriving Jewish community played an important role in the development of local industry and found success in business, education, and other professions. There were doctors and dentists, veterinarians and pharmacists, as well as a community of Jewish traders, peddlers, and skilled, prosperous workers. There were cattle dealers and tailors, leather workers and shoemakers, upholsterers and hat-makers, watchmakers and photographers, carpenters, kosher butchers, bakers, bankers, printers, and blacksmiths. There were companies specializing in textiles and construction, along with brickyards, transporters, beerhouses, and a distillery—all a testament to a burgeoning community that maintained a reasonable expectation for a bright future. An address book from 1930 lists my grandfather, Chaskel, as a tinsmith.

After the financial ruin of Germany in the wake of World War I, Hitler's nationalism appealed to an ever-broadening base, and what had sometimes been a subtle form of anti-Semitism was becoming more and more open and acceptable by society at large. Even though Jews had fought in the armies of Germany, Poland, and other countries during World War I, Jews were once again becoming an easy scapegoat on which to lay blame for Germany's woes. The situation for European Jews had always been tenuous, and whatever success they had achieved remained vulnerable.

Starachowice was at various times part of the Austrian and part of the Russian Partitions of Poland, but Poland regained independence in 1918, and by 1920, Starachowice was considered a major industrial center with the establishment of arms, artillery, and ammunition factories and ironworks facilities. The town of Starachowice was not actually established until April 1, 1939, when Wierzbnik merged with the settlement of Starachowice Fabryczne and the village known as Starachowice Gorne. The new town was known as Starachowice-Wierzbnik.

During the summer of 1939, my mother, my brother, and I traveled by train, leaving from the station at Skarzysko to Rabka Zdroj, between Krakow and Zakopane, to the mountains for a one-month vacation. Rabka, in a valley on the northern slopes of the Gorce Mountains with natural springs, is where the Rivers Poniczanka and Slonka intersect with the Raba River. Beginning in the latter half of the 19th century, Rabka became known for its salt works, and a children's treatment center specializing in hydrotherapy. It was also a popular spa destination in the 1930s, especially for Jews. My brother, Chaskel, was extremely skinny, and a doctor advised my mother to take him to Rabka to gain weight.

The Germans were closing in on Poland, but we were isolated, and news was scarce, so for that one month, my mother, my brother, and I shared a blissfully normal childhood summer experience. We went to the parks, rode horses, dressed in traditional Polish costumes, and took photographs. We enjoyed each other's company, and the tranquility of the countryside. We celebrated my ninth birthday. We did not know that it would be the last summer of peace for our family, for all of Poland, and for the world.

Perhaps my parents had a sense of the impending upheaval and tried to provide us with some sense of normalcy before the advent of war. They could not have fathomed the nearly total destruction of our culture, religion, country and *shtetl*. Perhaps when my mother, brother, and I were enjoying our time together in the mountains, my father was getting his affairs in order. If so, he did not let on to Chaskel or me. These were adult matters, and there was no need for children to involve themselves. My father eagerly awaited our return, and met us at the train station in Skarzysko, twenty miles from our home.

Even if my parents had been making preparations for changes that a war would bring, they did not discuss these adult matters with Chaskel or me. My grandparents told us stories about World War I, but no one could have imagined the horrors that lay ahead.

The ominous voice emanating from the radio recommended preparing for war. Two days later, on Friday, September 1, 1939, the Germans invaded Poland and reached our small town within a few days.

As the war began, we departed the town in a horse-drawn carriage. We initially thought the tanks rolling into Wierzbnik were English. We soon learned the horrible truth: they were German. As the horse and carriage clip-clopped along, the town of Wierzbnik disappeared behind us as we traveled to a farm in the countryside. Approximately eight kilometers away was a tiny settlement not appearing on any map. My grandparents called it Seszaw. My maternal grandparents, Maier and Ruchel Dawidowicz, had once owned property nearby and had gotten to know some of their Polish neighbors. My grandparents did not work the land themselves, but leased it to farmers. My grandfather, nicknamed Maier Seszaw, for the area in the countryside where my grandfather had his land, was in the business of brokering the purchase and sale of farm products and livestock, which he bought from Polish farmers and sold to Jewish butchers when he traveled into town, which he did at least twice a week. He was resourceful and entrepreneurial. He owned a horse and buggy and sold cloth and textiles and feathers for making pillows and comforters for the long Polish winters.

As the father of eight children, he built a large residential building in town with eight separate apartments, one for each of his children. On the ground-floor level were two storefronts, one for my grandfather, and one for his only son, my uncle Moishe.

When I was six years old, my grandparents sold their property in the countryside and moved to Wierzbnik full time. They lived at 53 Kolejowa Street, (Street of the Train), a few doors down from our house at 31 Kolejowa Street. The Street of the Train was not directly fronting the market square, but was a main artery in town with residential and commercial properties linking the main area of town with the train station, a vital link to the outside world, facilitating the exchange of people and goods.

My extended family was the circle of love that raised me, protected me, and taught me, especially about living Jewishly. But not all my family remained in our little corner of the world.

After World War I, my grandfather Maier's siblings and families emigrated to America. Two brothers settled in Canada, one brother went to New York City, and one sister went to Detroit. According to my grandfather Maier, "the new world of North America *wasn't kosher enough*," and to his great misfortune, he refused to join his siblings.

After the Germans invaded Wierzbnik, we stayed at the farm for just a few days. We had escaped to the relative security of the countryside. We later learned that the Germans did not want to conduct a massive bombing offensive in Starachowice, as the munitions factories were located there, and they knew these factories could be strategically vital to the war effort.

The war had arrived on our doorstep. We were no longer its neighbor. We were thrust into it, and it was thrust upon us. But who was this charismatic leader of Germany, the Fuhrer, who had whipped the populace into an anti-Semitic frenzy?

"When Jewish blood spills from the sword, all goes twice as well," Hitler declared. His anti-Semitic feelings were widely known. In 1920, Hitler wrote an article, "Why We Are Against the Jews." Hitler was determined to rid Germany of Jews, Gypsies, and the physically and mentally handicapped, as a way to cleanse Germany and to purify the Aryan race. In his 1925 and 1926 publications of *Mein Kampf,* he set out his hateful ideological program, stating that the Jews and the Bolsheviks were racially and ideologically inferior, even threatening, and encouraging a German revolution by the superior Aryans and National Socialists. His stated goals included the expulsion of the Jews from Germany and the unification of German people into one Greater Germany. Too many dismissed his ideas as the work of a madman.

Religious Jews with their *payos* and their traditional Hassidic garb, their isolationism, and their separation from mainstream society, were easy prey for xenophobic and disgruntled men and women who were easily brainwashed by the growing nationalistic Nazi movement. While they claimed ignorance to the goals of the Nazi regime, the population was aware of Nazism, and many openly supported their platform and believed its propaganda. There were Nazi-inspired board games and playing cards adorned with Hitler's image. There were anti-Jewish cartoons, slogans, and placards, and punishments for those who bought from Jewish-owned stores. The destruction of the European Jewish population did not happen overnight; it began with a series of anti-Semitic writings and speeches. And despite Jews being a part of life in Germany for over a thousand years, and having recently served in the German Army during World War I, Hitler declared, in 1933, that anyone with even one Jewish grandparent could no longer work with Aryans.

On November 7, 1938, Herschel Grynszpan, a seventeen-year-old Jew who had been sneaked into France and was living with extended family so as to avoid the increasing anti-Semitism in his native Germany, shot Ernst Vom Rath, a German diplomat in the Embassy in Paris. Grynszpan's parents and siblings were deported from Germany to Poland, along with thousands of other Jews whom Germany forced to "repatriate" to Poland. Grynszpan's family was caught in a no-man's land between the German and Polish borders and held in a refugee camp. Vom Rath died two days after being shot, triggering *Kristallnacht*, the Night of Broken Glass, when Germans torched Jewish businesses, synagogues, books, and Torahs, beginning, in earnest, their assault on Jews in Germany.

I was eight years old on *Kristallnacht* and blissfully unaware of it. If my parents ever discussed it, they were careful not to do so in front of Chaskel or me.

I was born at home on August 15, 1930, with the assistance of a midwife in Wierzbnik. My parents named me Michael (*Michulek*) Baranek, but I was affectionately referred to as *Michulciu*. I was the firstborn, the son of Jews from generations descended from Abraham. And just as Abraham sealed the covenant with God through circumcision, my parents fulfilled that same Jewish tradition when I was eight days old. In Europe, this was a clear way to identify a Jewish boy or man. Two years later, my brother Chaskel was born, and he too would have a *bris*.

My paternal grandparents were Chaskel and Leah Baranek. My grandfather, a tinsmith, passed away when I was a year old. When my brother was born a year after that, my parents named him in memory of my deceased grandfather. As was common in this era, especially among the small Jewish gene pool, my grandmothers, Leah Baranek and Ruchel Davidowicz, were distant relatives.

During the summers, my mother's extended family spent time at my grandfather's farm, with all the cousins and siblings. From my grandfather's seven daughters and one son, he was blessed with sixteen grandchildren. One could only imagine the number of family members gathered around the table at a Passover Seder, had those grandchildren lived to produce families of their own, but alas only two of the fifteen grandchildren survived the Nazis, and I am one of them.

In those times, families engaged a matchmaker to bring a potential groom to meet a bride's family. It was expensive to marry, and my grandfather had seven daughters! A woman needed to have a dowry to offer the groom. Times were changing and this custom was beginning to fall out of fashion. Only my mother's older sisters had a *shiddach*, or an arranged marriage. The younger sisters were still single. In those days, it was more prestigious to have a mid-week wedding. The ceremony always took place outside under a *chuppah*, the marriage canopy, and the wedding reception was usually held at one's home where special cooks were hired to prepare food for the wedding reception. The celebration typically included a *klezmer* band, made up of a violin player, a clarinet player, a trumpeter, and a drummer. It was quite traditional. One of my aunts was married on Saturday, a "quiet wedding," because of the many restrictions on how one could celebrate on the Sabbath. Many of these old-fashioned customs were going out of style, especially in large, modern cities, but Wierzbnik was a small, traditional town.

My father, Moszek "Moishe" Ber Baranek, a tall man with a generous nature, was a merchant in the business of buying and selling steel, hardware, building supplies, and farming equipment. He had a license to sell certain specialized items for his equipment business in the area encompassing Seszaw. He imported some materials from the town of Oswiecim, (known in German as Auschwitz). My father employed both Jews and non-Jews. As was a typical setup in Europe, my father owned a building with commercial space on the street level and residences above. He also built and owned a separate warehouse nearby. Our home was large. My mother, Chaja Dawidowicz, owned and operated a grocery store in one of the ground floor commercial spaces. Groceries were sold in bulk. Nothing was pre-packaged, and almost everything was perishable. The two most sought after commodities at the time were sugar and soap. My mother was a small woman, attractive and hardworking. She knew most of her customers and sold to them mostly on credit. She was a busy woman, running a household and a business. For country folk, my parents were making their way in the world, improving their circumstances, and beginning to elevate themselves.

The building that housed the commercial space downstairs and residences above was divided between my father and his brother, Ben Zion. On our side of the building lived my immediate family, my parents, Chaskel, and me. Our live-in Polish maid spoke Yiddish fluently, rare for a non-Jew. Above the store were two apartments that my parents rented out, one to the Rabinovich family, the other to the Gutterman family. On my uncle's side of the building lived my uncle and his wife, Sala, and their daughter, Nacha, born in 1940, when I was ten. My uncle rented one of his spare apartments to non-Jews, also a rarity at the time.

Our town was a mix of traditional Jewish families and Catholic Poles. A church with a steeple rose high above the town. The town square was ringed with homes and businesses, government buildings, and the train station. Near our house was a small statue of Christian significance, likely honoring a saint, standing about four feet high. When there was a Catholic funeral procession, we would close our doors and shutters, not out of superstition about death, but so as not to call attention to our status as Jewish outsiders in a Catholic country. Although there was relative peace in our community between Christians and Jews, there was always an overriding awareness of *us* and *them*. Despite their successes and accomplishments, Jews throughout history have long known their place in society: others, strangers, outsiders.

My family worked hard and was comfortable financially. My father continually sought to better himself in many ways. His first language was Yiddish and he spoke Polish with a detectable accent, but his desire to progress in business with his many non-Jewish customers led him to hire a private tutor to help him improve his Polish grammar and pronunciation.

Wierzbnik was a *shtetl*, a small town. It was not as small as some of the remote villages, where town criers announced the news, but not so large as Warsaw or Krakow, which had streetcars. Our town also had a train station, which would prove to be both a blessing and a curse for the people of Wierzbnik. The streets of Wierzbnik were lined with cobblestones. Some homes had electricity; others did not. We were among the fortunate few who had electricity, but we did not have running water or indoor bathrooms. Behind our house was an outhouse. It was a structure with three separate stalls, one for each of the living quarters within our side of the building. There was no toilet paper in those days, so people in towns used newspapers to clean themselves; however, in the countryside and on farms, people only had leaves at their disposal.

Because we had no running water, we had a few white enamel containers, two to three feet high, that we used to store well-water. *Treigers*, water carriers, earned their living by transporting water for household use. Water carriers would deliver water from the well in the market square to our house a few times a week. There were other wells around town, but the one in the town square had a reputation for purity. The water carriers would draw water from the well in pails, attached to the ends of a shoulder yoke. This wooden device would rest on the water carrier's neck and shoulders. Water was heated on the stove to use for cooking or to fill a bathtub. Typically, we bathed Thursday evenings, or on Fridays, in preparation for Shabbat. Customarily, the man of the house bathed first, followed by the woman of the house, and then the children. Water was costly and so had to be used sparingly. There was a *mikve* in town, but that was only used for ritual bathing and purification, and in principle, not for hygiene. Household water was not used for cleaning clothes either, as well-water was too valuable for such use. The maid would carry the laundry to the river and clean the clothes there. We used wood and coal to heat our home and our stove. Fortunately, we had a wood or coal-burning heater in each bedroom. Poland was cold much of the year, and even during the summer, temperatures dropped at night.

One of our prized possessions was a large radio. We gathered around the radio to listen to various programs, including the weekly broadcast from Jerusalem. Often, my father would situate the radio near the window facing the street, so that others who did not own a radio could listen, too. He especially did this when it was becoming apparent that the political situation in Germany was worsening, and that war was imminent. The impending doom was palpable. We received daily copies of Jewish newspapers from Warsaw, but the deliveries ceased when the war broke out.

Life was simple during my fleeting childhood. When I was five years old, the former dictator of Poland, Josef Pilsudski, died. The Jews of Wierzbnik mourned his death, as it ended a period of relative safety and stability for Jews in Poland. Pilsudski's regime was favorable to ethnic minorities, including Jews, because Pilsudski was more interested in an individual's loyalty to the state, to Poland, than to any particular ethnic or religious group. Many Jews supported Pilsudski, who attempted to restrain anti-Semitic sentiment in Poland. He maintained public order, even though there were certainly anti-Semitic acts. Jews were prohibited, for example, from working in the armament factories in Starachowice. Pilsudski's death signaled a general downturn in the stability of Jewish life in Poland. Anti-Semitism spread like wildfire across the Polish countryside – fast and unstoppable.

At the age of seven, I entered school, but only had two years of formal Polish public school education as a result of the unfortunate circumstance of the war. Chaskel received no formal education, but he did receive a Jewish education. By the time he was old enough to attend regular Polish school, Jews were already forbidden from attending.

Throughout eastern Europe, most Jews were observant; however, the Reform movement, which began in the 1800s, was taking root in more populated cities throughout Europe, especially in Germany where it began. Regardless of denomination, however, nearly every Jew kept kosher, observed the Sabbath, and studied Torah. Nearly every Jewish family sent their sons to *cheder*, a school to learn Hebrew and study Torah. *Cheders* were common throughout Europe. Lessons were often taught by a *melamed*, a teacher. Parents paid the *melamed* directly for the Hebrew and Torah classes. We often studied by the light of a kerosene lamp. The *cheder* was in the basement of the building across the street from our home; I could walk there, as to most places in town. We felt safe in our town, and Chaskel and I were free to walk around as we pleased.

Although I knew my non-Jewish classmates in Polish school, I could not count them among my friends. We sat two to a desk in our classes, but non-Jews never wanted to sit with us. They taunted us, saying that we smelled like onions and, due to our diet, heavily laden with onions, perhaps we did! This could have been general childhood banter, and not something more sinister, but that anti-Semitic sentiment was learned somewhere, and throughout Poland's history, these attitudes were often taught at home, as well as in church. Aside from such small incidents, I do not recall any outward anti-Semitism intended for my family or me in particular. There were, however, boycott days, when some Poles refused to buy from Jewish stores. I don't know if my mother's store was ever targeted before the war, but this may have just been my youthful naïveté, or just the acceptance that this was something that Jews should expect. Jewish students who desired to study in Polish universities were required to stand, rather than to sit at a desk, but this was as it had always been; it was the reality of being a Jew in a country that was no friend of the Jews. Anti-Semitism was standard practice. As Jews, we knew our place in society, so when anti-Semitic acts or taunts increased in small increments, it was not so noticeable.

Every once in a while my family would go to the local movie theater, which played silent and talking pictures. The cinema, as well as our town, was integrated, but there was always a sense of separation between Jews and non-Jews. We recognized Poles from our town, and they recognized us, but any interaction was purely businesslike, not personal.

The Jewish community supported live theater and an array of visiting entertainers who performed in Yiddish. The circus came to Wierzbnik to perform, and I remember seeing a black man for the first time. We were isolated and sheltered in our upbringing and had little experience with the world outside our small town.

Although we were not as religious as some local families, or even as observant as my grandparents, our lives revolved around the Jewish calendar. The rhythm of our lives centered around Shabbat, and other Jewish holidays. In addition to Rosh Hashanah and Yom Kippur, my family celebrated other major holidays, including Pesach (Passover), and Sukkot. The maid helped my mother prepare for Shabbat, buying the meat, fish, candles, and other items for the weekly meal. My mother baked her own *challah* and prepared a chopped, sweet fish for Shabbat dinner. We would bathe and wear our finest clothes for Shabbat. Family members living in other towns or cities tended to travel to celebrate major holidays with one another. In preparation for Pesach, my mother rid the house of *chametz,* which included anything leaven. The night before the Seder (the ceremonial dinner when the *Hagaddah,* the story of the Hebrews' liberation from slavery in Egypt, is retold each spring), my father would take a feather and a candle, searching for any last *chametz.* If any was found, it would be burned, as was tradition.

"Purim is not a *Yom Tov,* and malaria is not a sickness" was one of those expressive Yiddish sayings I often heard in our house and around town. Although Purim is not considered a major holiday, we followed the tradition of *shlacha mones.* My mother, sometimes with the help of our maid, would prepare *hamantashen,* traditional three-pointed cookies filled with prunes, apricots, or other fillings. They would arrange the sweets in a beautiful presentation on china plates that we delivered to family and friends around town.

Although we had a synagogue in town, the *Bet Midrash*, people tended to follow a specific rabbi, regardless of where he resided. The *Bet Midrash* had a *yeshiva* attached to it where "day students" studied Torah. Local families welcomed these students into their homes for meals. Some families with means even gave traveling students a place to spend the night.

Many people prayed and gathered for their holidays in their local *shtiebel*. Every *shtiebel* had its own *Sefer Torah,* a scroll handwritten by a scribe under exacting requirements. The Torah, containing the five books of Moses, is the cornerstone of the Jewish religion and the holiest of its books. The *Sefer Torah* was used for prayer services during the week and on *Shabbat*. During my youth, the *shtiebel* that my family attended was a fair walk from our house, but, during the ghetto period, my grandmother, known throughout the community for her generosity, let the community use a room in her home as a *shtiebel*. The spiritual leader who guided some families from our community was Rabbi Yosele of Wochock, from the neighboring city of Radom. Other families followed other rabbis and they worshipped in their own *shtiebels*. Before major holidays, my father would travel by train to Radom to seek out special blessings from the rabbi, and to take money to the rabbi for his support.

Although our town was not as sophisticated as Warsaw or other large cities, it was not a primitive *shtetl* either. There was a Jewish doctor and a Jewish dentist, and a few other professionals in our town. They were educated elsewhere, as Wierzbnik did not have a university. Dr. Leon Kurta, our dentist, filled my cavities with some kind of cement. Later, we heard rumors that people were having dentists fill their teeth with gold and diamonds as a way of ensuring that they had something of value on their bodies, in case things continued to get worse. Shimon or "Shimmale," as he was affectionately known, was our local shoemaker. Growing up, I took my shoes for granted. Only later would I realize the value of a proper pair of shoes, and long for the days when Shimmale would carefully measure our feet and expertly craft our shoes from fine leather. While visiting his shop, Shimon would speak about his devoutly communist views. As time went on, we realized that espousing one's political views was also becoming more dangerous. Openly opposing the German government, the dictatorship of the Fuhrer, was cause for alarm, and could mean almost certain imprisonment or death. Soon, however, simply being Jewish made one a target of the Nazis and also resulted in imprisonment or death.

To everyone's surprise, especially to the Poles, the Germans rapidly overpowered the Polish army. In a matter of a few short days, during which we remained in the countryside, the Germans occupied Wierzbnik. Upon our return, we learned that the local school had become German headquarters. We saw ominous Nazi flags flying from government buildings all over town. I gazed upon the German soldiers, marveling at their high black leather boots. It was exciting, but frightening, to see the soldiers in their smart military garb, and to see and hear their trucks and motorcycles in our previously quiet town.

During World War I, my grandfather, Maier, had lived on his farm, a *rzepin,* which could be seen from the main road. It had a straw roof and a wood oven for heating. There was a barn with some animals. During the First World War, my grandfather housed a German commandant at the farm and spoke of him kindly and with respect. When the Germans invaded Poland in 1939, my grandfather thought that things would improve for the Jews. Little did he know that these Germans, these Nazis, were radically different from the Germans of the First World War.

German occupation of our town brought fear and insecurity that we had not known previously. The Nazis imposed a curfew of 6:00 p.m. and implemented restrictions on Jews, including prohibiting the use of public transportation. A Jew was required to remove his hat in the presence of German officers. A Jew had to walk in the street, rather than on the sidewalk. And so began the slow torments of humiliation and degradation. Every day brought a new edict, a new restriction on our liberty. At first, these rules seemed rather benign, as they were enacted incrementally. By the time the Jewish community realized we had lost our freedom, our rights, our possessions, and our communities, it was too late.

The Germans established a police force in Wierzbnik. There were the regular police, charged with law enforcement in rural and urban areas, and the Gestapo, or security police, charged with overseeing political crimes.

German anti-Semitism was immediately apparent. We knew that we, not Poland, were the targets of the German war effort. After taking over the town, the Germans imprisoned a number of Jews, who were later freed. Others were consigned to forced labor and made to clear and clean the streets from the destruction caused by the bombing. Poles began shunning their Jewish neighbors and ousting them from bread lines. Food and other supplies became scarce. A few weeks into the German occupation, on the eve of *Yom Kippur*, the Germans broke into the synagogue, beat many of the Jews, and forced them into the streets before setting the synagogue ablaze. Like the ancient Temple in Jerusalem, our synagogue lay in ruins.

Just a few weeks after the German invasion, on September 17, 1939, the Soviet Army invaded Poland from the east. Little by little, our country was being overrun from all directions. It became painfully clear to adults that we were not Polish, but Jews that the Poles had permitted to live upon their soil. We were trapped from all sides, with no opportunity to escape. We children were less aware of the political forces surrounding us, but we sensed the increasing restrictions on our once carefree childhoods.

For a short time, the local school was closed, and when it reopened, no Jews were permitted to attend. Jews were forced to turn over their radios, fur coats, jewelry, and other valuables. Even the Poles were forced to turn over their radios and possessions. My brother and I had bicycles, but for unknown reasons, the Germans never confiscated them, as they had in other cities. German soldiers searched the homes of Jews to ensure that the mandates of the Third Reich were followed. Ever so gradually, our rights and movements were taken away.

The mail stopped operating, and the Jewish newspapers were no longer delivered from Warsaw. This, along with the requirement to turn in our radios, led to isolation. Our communication with the outside world came to a halt.

My parents did not make much of turning in the radio. They said, "*There are bigger things to worry about.*" They were likely trying to hide their fears from my brother and me, and perhaps it concerned them a little less, as they did not face the humiliation of personally turning over their possessions. My father simply hired a *treiger*, a porter, to deliver whatever material possessions were demanded by the Germans. In many ways, during this early period of the war, life went on fairly normally for us.

Our inability to attend school was, of course, a big change in our daily routine. My parents hired a tutor to teach my brother and me. Mostly, we studied Polish with the tutor, who had been relocated from Lodz to Wierzbnik. It must have been difficult to keep two young boys entertained when we could not comprehend the greater situation, and were prohibited not only from attending school but also from engaging in normal childhood activities.

Gradually, the situation in our city, and throughout Poland, worsened. One day, my grandfather, Maier, arrived at home shaken up: "*Zayde*, what happened to you?"

He answered with a quivering voice. "I was walking down the street, lost in thought, but aware of the presence of some Germans. The next thing I knew, they grabbed me and held me down. There was a struggle, and when I finally freed myself, I realized they had cut half of my beard."

"What will you do now, *zayde*? Will you shave the other side?"

"No, my dear boy, I am a religious man. I will cover my face with a handkerchief until it grows back."

This aggressive act by the Germans, on a public street, was meant to intimidate and caused my grandfather great embarrassment. We felt his shame, but were grateful that nothing worse had happened to him. We were beginning to learn to what extent the Germans would go in punishing Jews. On one occasion, four people from our town were taken away. Caskets containing ashes (presumably of the four) returned. People were in shock, asking *what kind of civilized people would do such a thing?* We were beginning to learn what kind of people could do such things: everyday people easily led by the Nazi machine, people who conformed in order to protect themselves, or to get ahead. The Germans' random acts of violence horrified the Jews of Wierzbnik who, like so many other Polish Jews, were hard-working, God-fearing, peace-loving people.

Before the war, Wierzbnik had some four thousand non-Jews, and eight hundred Jewish families. At the start of the war, the Jewish population had risen to roughly three thousand six hundred Jews, and fluctuated throughout the war based upon various transports from other *shtetls* and towns. Trains carrying Jews from Lodz arrived in Wierzbnik on March 2, 1940 and March 13, 1940; another train carrying Jews arrived from Plock in March 1941.

On November 23, 1939, a *Judenrat* was established, along with a fifteen-member Jewish police force charged with keeping order within the Jewish community. The *Judenrat* (or *Gminna*, as it was called in Polish and Yiddish) consisted of members of the previous community council, headed by Symcha Mintzberg and Moishe Birencweig. The Germans required the *Judenrat* to raise one hundred thousand *zloty* and to provide approximately three to four hundred able-bodied men for forced labor for the Third Reich. These laborers were sent to work in surrounding villages. My father managed to avoid these forced labor assignments, probably because of his connections or contributions to the *Judenrat*.

In early 1940, the Nazis ordered all adult Jews to wear a white armband with a blue Star of David or the word *"Jude"* on it. When this law was enacted, people felt the pain of degradation. The arm-band, which Jews had to make themselves, was to be worn at all times when outside one's home. I was too young to have to wear one, but I remember that adult Jews wore them until deportations to the concentration camps began.

Amidst the tumult and uncertainty, life continued: people married, babies were born, other life-cycle events occurred, and I turned ten.

THE WIERZBNIK GHETTO

ON APRIL 2, 1941, the Jewish ghetto of Wierzbnik, consisting of six to eight blocks of housing, was established. Our house lay within the boundaries of the ghetto, but my mother's store was closed because it was impossible to get supplies. Staying in our own home, in familiar surroundings, did much to keep our morale up. My mother's sister's family of five – Leibel and his wife, Mirel, and their children, Moishe, Mattes, and Gucia Szpagats – lived in Wierzbnik, but their house was outside the boundaries of the ghetto. When the Szpagats were forced from their home, my parents took them in. They lived with us until the evacuation of our town. My maternal grandparents' house, being up the street from ours, also lay within the ghetto boundaries, and they, too, were able to remain in their familiar surroundings. (Moishe was the only cousin of mine from that side of my family who survived the war. We are the only two survivors among my maternal grandparents' grandchildren).

Unlike other ghettos established throughout the Third Reich, there were no physical walls surrounding the Wierzbnik Ghetto. Still, there were signs demarcating the boundaries. The ghetto marked the beginning of our psychological imprisonment.

In 1940, Walther Becker was transferred from Hamburg, Germany, to Starachowice. Becker had served in the German Army during World War I, after which, in 1920, he joined the Hamburg police force, receiving civil service status as a criminal investigator. He joined the Nazi Party in 1937, and became a member of the Criminal Police *(Krminalpolizei or Kripo),* attached to the Security Police *(Sicherheitspolizei or Sipo).* He took command of the Sipo station when his superior was transferred out of Starachowice, and received a rank equivalent to that of a member of the *Schutzstaffel, or* "SS," which was not uncommon for non-SS Germans holding important occupation positions throughout Eastern Europe. We had heard, or thought or assumed, that he was a member of the *Sicherheitsdienst des Reichsfuhrers*, "SD," the intelligence agency of the SS. We had no idea that his application for general membership in the SS had been rejected, so he would certainly never have been a member of the elite SD, but Becker's rank and status within the Third Reich were of no consequence to us. All that mattered was that Becker was the highest-ranking German in our town, the one who wielded power, which he exercised at random.

Although Jews were not allowed to voluntarily leave the ghetto, Poles were permitted to enter. This provided Jews an opportunity to buy food and other supplies. A thriving black market helped the Jewish community of Wierzbnik remain relatively strong and healthy, at least for a while. For those in need, the *Judenrat* established a soup kitchen to provide some six hundred meals each day. The ISS, a Jewish self-help organization based in Krakow, assisted the *Judenrat* with funds to operate this soup kitchen.

There was a curfew in the ghetto. No one was allowed out after dark. The Jewish police enforced the curfew, but would not have killed someone for breaking it. The Germans certainly would have, though it was rare that the SS or Germans would venture into the ghetto at night, and nobody within the ghetto dared stray from their homes after dark.

Our house was a stone's throw away from the *Gminna*, the Jewish Council. There were always people coming and going, so we were well-positioned to hear the latest news. There was also a central board where announcements were posted on the *Gminna* building. This also informed us of new developments.

My family was lucky in that we were not greatly affected by food shortages in pre-ghetto days, and even after the ghetto was established, because my parents had connections with Poles who assisted us. One night, the German police came to arrest my father, but thankfully an acquaintance of my father, a local Polish policeman, had tipped him off and my father fled before the Germans arrived at our door. I can only assume that my mother knew of my father's hideout. Or perhaps he withheld this information from her so that she could not confess it if pressed by the Germans to do so. She did not say whether she was frightened by this incident, and if she was afraid, she did not show it in front of Chaskel or me. She was a woman of great strength.

We were all relieved when my father returned unharmed the following day. My parents' acquaintances with non-Jews helped us in small but important ways. I am certain this assistance was not solely out of the goodness of the non-Jews' hearts, but because my parents were able to financially compensate them. Somehow my father continued to work to some extent, and to keep up his business relationships and contacts with Poles outside the ghetto.

Periodically there would be a *revizia*, a daytime search of one's home, typically by two German guards. My father would usually be informed in advance by the local Polish police or by the *Gminna*, so we would have some warning. My parents would have me wear two pairs of pants. In the first pair, I would hide valuables in the pockets: jewelry, U.S. dollars, or gold coins. Then I would don a second pair of pants. In case anyone asked me to empty my pockets, the outer pants' pockets would be empty. My parents knew they could trust me to remain calm and to keep my wits in case of a raid. The two years that separated my brother and me were critical during these times. My brother was too young to keep his composure the same way I did. From an early age, I knew that when things got tough, you either had to sharpen up, or you were finished. Perhaps I learned that from my parents, who never panicked during these searches. They remained calm, probably for all our sakes, but likely because they believed in the war's limits. They could not have imagined 850,000 Jews would be murdered at Treblinka, beginning in July 1942, in the space of less than a year. Or that millions more Jews would be murdered in Majdanek, Auschwitz-Birkenau, Mauthausen, Bergen-Belsen, Thereisenstadt, and in other locations, known and unknown, during the *Shoah*. It is estimated that six million Jews perished during the Holocaust, but the exact number will never be known with certainty. The Germans were very detailed record-keepers, so we do know with certainty the numbers of those killed in the camps or during actions for which the Germans kept logs. Who could have believed that so many would collaborate in the systematic killing of innocent people? My parents probably thought things would be bad for a while, as they had been during the First World War, but then the war would end, and things would return to normal, or at least to some kind of post-war normal. This war, with this evil regime, changed everything.

Historically, the town square, or *rynek*, in any European town was the center of activity. During the ghetto period, half of the square was within the designated ghetto and the other half was outside. There was no physical boundary that guided us, but we knew where the line was and dared not cross it. Thankfully the well in the town square known to have the purest water was on the ghetto side, so we were allowed access to water. Although there were other wells in the ghetto, we preferred to get water from the town square. Fortunately, even during the ghetto period, water *treigers* would deliver water to our house.

The Germans were unpredictable, and this kept everyone in the ghetto on edge. Once, the SS stormed into the *Gminna* near our house, and in an unprovoked attack, viciously beat some of the *Gminna* members. Who knows why. Maybe they wanted to instill fear; maybe they were just full of rage and hatred. *Just carrying out orders?* Despite the fact that the Jewish Police headquarters were just downstairs from the *Gminna,* the Jewish police were helpless to aid their fellow Jews. There was no fighting against the Germans, the Nazis, the SS, who were oppressing us. They attacked or shot anyone in sight, without consequence; they tortured or killed as they pleased.

Not far from the house of my friend, Howard Chandler, near the town square, some German soldiers were patrolling the streets, when a soldier of the *Krajowa Army* (the Polish Land Army) shot and wounded one of the Germans. In retaliation, the Germans rounded up sixteen or seventeen of the accused gunman's family, including women, to be executed. To foment animosity between the Poles and the Jews, the Germans ordered the *Gminna* to prepare gallows in the market square. The Germans were forcing the Jews to do their dirty work, to turn them into executioners. The Jewish community, fearing more reprisals from the Polish community, raised enough money to bribe the Germans to permit the executioners to wear masks. In this way, the Poles would not know who carried out the hangings and would be less likely to retaliate against individuals. The Germans encouraged all to attend the hanging, over which Walther Becker presided. On a Sunday morning, the last day of August 1941, just two weeks after my eleventh birthday, as the church bells rang, dismissing the local Christian Poles from their nearby church, the accused were hanged in the market square. Everyone was gathered in the square, Jews and Poles alike. I felt a strange energy that day, a perverse excitement in the air. I had never witnessed a hanging before, had never seen someone killed so close in proximity. As I walked by the bodies, I looked up to see the engorged faces of the condemned, some with their tongues protruding. The bodies were left swinging from the gallows for an entire day until they were stiff. They were left to terrorize the community, and to forewarn against further attempts to fight back against the Germans, who tried to deepen the divide between the Polish and the Jewish populations in every way possible. It seemed that the Germans were amused by the public spectacle of the hanging.

The hanging seemed to bring about the effect the Germans were hoping for, as it seemed there were few if any attempts to strike back at the Germans in our town after that day.

The previous year, in 1940, the Germans required all Jewish males up to the age of forty-five to register for work. They sent many to forced labor camps near Lublin. The yoke of the German occupation began to intensify. I had a permit to work on the roads, laying stones, which at least allowed me to get a ration card, which I gave my mother. The items she got in the shops would be marked off the card. In this small way, I was able to help my family.

Over a three-year period, our rights and freedoms diminished. Rumors abounded about the fate of Jews in other places, but there was no route of escape: The Germans occupied Poland and the surrounding European countries, and the Russians were advancing from the east. Transportation was slow, by horse-drawn carriage, by walking, or, for the wealthy, by train. And even if one had transportation, where could one go? There was no safety in any direction any longer, and papers, legal or otherwise, were hard to come by.

No one could grasp the enormity of it all, or fathom the number of Jews and non-Jews who were being killed, and who would yet be killed. The Germans tightened the noose around the neck of the eastern European Jewish community so slowly, that by the time one realized what was happening, it was too late. Young adults without wives or children were able to escape to the forest. Those with children or with established businesses, and those who were elderly or infirm, were unlikely or unable to uproot themselves and flee.

There were two main Polish underground forces: The *Krajowa Army ("AK")*, the Land Army, notoriously anti-Semitic, and, *Ludowa,* the People's Army (*"AL"*), supported by the Russians. *Ludowa* allowed Jews to serve in its ranks. It was a huge risk to flee to the forest, or anywhere, as there was always the risk that one would run into the *AK* first, rather than the *AL*.

My parents took certain actions in preparation for the unknown, but continued to try to make our lives seem normal. My mother gave some of our possessions, including our family photographs, to their non-Jewish neighbors, the Spytkowskis, to hold during the war. We all sensed that our days in Wierzbnik were nearing an end.

My parents sat us down and spoke to us in a straightforward manner: With my mother looking on, my father turned to my brother and said, "Chaskel, with your blue eyes, you could easily pass as a Pole. We have made arrangements for you to be taken for safekeeping with a Polish family. We hope that this will only be temporary, but Wierzbnik no longer feels as safe as it once had, and we cannot take any chances. You will only be able to take a few possessions with you. You will have to try to blend in as a Pole, and as a part of their family. They are taking a big risk by agreeing to do this, but we must trust that all will be okay. They will come to collect you on October 26th."

But they never arrived. Did they take the money without ever intending to "adopt" Chaskel, or were their efforts foiled by a tightening German noose? Perhaps they had heard of the impending liquidation of the Wierzbnik Ghetto and feared for their own safety. Jewish Ghettos throughout Poland, in Lublin, Warsaw, Radom, and in smaller towns, had already been *cleared*. Certainly, Poles with freedom of movement and access to news were aware of the disappearing Jewish communities. Poles jeopardized their own lives when hiding Jews. Whether they took the risk for the money, or whether they were truly altruistic, if the Germans had found the Polish family hiding Chaskel, a Jew, the Germans would not hesitate to kill them or send them to a concentration camp.

Others from our town were making arrangements to hide their children if possible. My father's close friend, Yaakov Yitzhak Milman, who attended the same *shtiebel*, and his wife, Rojza, owned a bakery which was aryanized by a German named Otto Bastian. In a desperate attempt to save his children, Yaakov paid a police detective named Tomczyk to hide his two daughters and one son. But the worst fears of the family were realized when, two days later, rather than harboring the Milman children as Tomczyk had promised in exchange for a bribe, he shot the children dead in the marketplace in cold blood. There was no recourse for the Jews who suffered so terribly at the hands of the Germans, as well as at the hands of some of our Polish neighbors. Offering a bribe to a Pole, or to anyone, was a risk. But often risks had to be taken to ensure day-to-day survival. Survival was random.

I remember one particular member of the Order Police, or *Gendarmerie*, named Ertel, who we referred to as *"Nasel"* or *"Nozek"* *("The Nose")*. He was known to grab a Jew every Friday it seemed, took him out of the ghetto, and shot him in the woods. The unpredictability of it all was maddening, and drove many to the brink of insanity.

Around the same time as my parents made arrangements to hide Chaskel, my aunt and uncle made the agonizing decision to send my two-year-old cousin, Nacha, (later known as Nora), to Warsaw, with a non-Jew, to hide her. It is unknown when the entrusted Pole sent Nacha to a convent, but according to what the family was able to learn, Nacha was put in a basket in front of a church and, at some later date, was sent to a convent in France, where she remained for the duration of the war.

People were sending their children into hiding, storing valuable possessions in obscure hiding places, making arrangements the best they could for an unknown eventuality. There was an increasing intensity and palpable fear among the Jewish population in the ghetto. My father owned a warehouse near our house that he used for business. He also owned vacant land, where he gathered natural materials to be sold to a brick-maker. The town was abuzz with talk of resettlements.

"Michulciu, come, follow me to the warehouse," said my father, and I followed close behind him. "Look here and remember well, my son. I have buried some of our valuables, silver and candelabras in this spot. If we are forced to leave Wierzbnik, these precious items will be waiting for us upon our return. They will be here for safekeeping. This is between us. You understand? It is better that you do not share this information with anyone, not even Chaskel. I can trust you to keep this secret, but your brother is still young and may not be able to hold his tongue. This is serious, Michulciu, and I am counting on you to remember where these valuables are hidden in case you need to retrieve them one day."

We were fortunate to remain in our own house and to have means to obtain food and trade for necessities. Others were less fortunate, especially those from outside Wierzbnik. The poor, and those forced to do hard labor, did not fare well. Life went on in the ghetto, and so too, death. People died of natural causes, at the hands of the Germans, or at the hands of their Polish, Ukranian or other accomplices. The Jewish cemetery, where my grandfather was buried in 1931, was outside the ghetto boundaries. To prevent diseases from spreading, able-bodied Jewish men were granted permission to leave the ghetto to bury the dead in the cemetery. Toward the end of the ghetto period and after the war began, an unmarked mass grave at the edge of the cemetery was filled with corpses. No one said *Kaddish*, (the mourner's prayer), for those poor souls. No headstones identified the dead or marked their final resting spot.

Two work camps operated near Wierzbnik. One produced munitions; the other was a woodworking mill. These factories employed Poles from other towns, until 1939 when Jewish forced labor began to be used instead. Through connections, my mother obtained work permits: one for herself at the woodworking mill, and one for my father at the munitions factory. Many believed that the Jews of Wierzbnik, at least a few, would be saved because the factories were essential to the German war effort. The forced labor was valuable, and thus these *lucky* Jews were more useful alive than dead.

My father's uncle in Warsaw, Maier Baranek, had three sons, all well-educated. One of the sons, my father's cousin, Motek, smuggled photographs out of the Warsaw Ghetto, and got them to our house.

The middle son, Juzek, an engineer, came to Wierzbnik when matters worsened in Warsaw. Juzek was able to get a permit to work in the camp at Starachowice, but when an explosion occurred one day at the factory, Juzek was accused of sabotage. He was arrested, and sent to a jail for Jewish prisoners. My father tried to get Juzek released, but was unable to bribe any of the guards. An inability to bribe the guards indicated that things were getting ever more serious, and that neither education, nor financial means, ensured one's safety. The youngest son, Beniek, stayed in Warsaw with his parents and brother, Motek. They remained in the Warsaw ghetto until they were sent for "resettlement," in Treblinka, the death camp where all four were killed.

In early October 1942, two cousins from Ostrowiec, Tilczia and Wowciu "Volf" Weinberg, arrived to stay with my grandparents. The two were children of my mother's sister, Chana, and her husband, Abraham. Ostrowiec, a town some thirty kilometers from Wierzbnik, had a factory that made train cars. For a while, the Jews living there were somewhat protected, as their jobs also aided the war effort, similar to the work camps in Starachowice. But time was running out for all, as the reach of the Third Reich grew.

There was tension in the warm autumn air. The incremental tugging at our freedom had been building up for a while, and we sensed change was afoot. The unknown brought constant worry. We had heard rumors of entire Jewish communities being resettled and then never being heard from again. The war was waging, and the Germans were continuing their assault on one European country after another. Without newspapers or the freedom to travel, without normal interaction, and without the ability to listen to the radio or receive regular mail, we lacked reliable information about what was happening. Given the scarcity of food and other essentials, we were truly more concerned with our day-to-day existence than what was happening beyond our little corner of the world. My parents still tried to shield us from the reality of what they knew and how our plight was deteriorating. I assume they knew more than they let on to us children, but again, whatever they heard, were only tales, but I sensed that it did not bode well for us when my father was unable to bribe the police to release his cousin, Juzek, or when the Polish family failed to show up to claim Chaskel.

In the early morning hours of October 27, 1942, the sixteenth day of *Cheshvan*, before the sun had risen, the Jewish police ordered everyone to the marketplace with whatever belongings they could carry in one small bag. This was the day that we feared most, the day that would prove the most pivotal for the Jewish community of Wierzbnik, and for me personally. The life I had known ended that day with the destruction of my community and the only life I had ever known. It was the end of innocence. The end of my sheltered existence. The end of the regular cycles of weekly Shabbats and other holidays and festival celebrations shared with loved ones. It was the moment that marked the finality of my childhood innocence with the awakening of the notion that the potential for brutality and violence lives within the heart of each human being. This was the moment when all our collective illusions were shattered. We had deluded ourselves as a community and as a family only in order to get through each day. Now, the truth of our terrible destiny was only too real. The morning of the Great Aktzia, I awoke in my bed, in my home with my family. By day's end, the Jewish community of Wierzbnik would exist no longer, and neither would the Baraneks, as the family I had once known.

Some with connections in the *Gminna* were warned the previous night of the liquidation, and hurried to some of the work camps to avoid being in Wierzbnik during the liquidation of the ghetto the next morning. This time my father had not received such advance notice.

Sipo Commander Walther Becker led the operation, aided by German police and Ukrainian and Lithuanian guards. Polish police, wielding whips and accompanied by vicious attack dogs, surrounded the ghetto. They fired shots into the air as a warning. Nearly five thousand Jews were herded into the marketplace.

In all, some ninety-eight Jews were shot and killed on the day of the liquidation, including some Jews who were caught hiding or those who were too old or otherwise physically unable to walk to the marketplace. The guards shot them on sight for not having appeared at the marketplace. The sound of the shots, and the chaos that ensued, caused disorientation and panic.

On the morning of the Great Aktzia, when the entire ghetto population was deported, all in our house – my parents, my grandmother, my aunts and uncles and cousins, my brother, and I – dressed hastily. We put a few things in a backpack, including containers of water, where our parents had secured some money in false bottoms. They had anticipated our needs in case of emergency. We left the house that morning, leaving everything in its place. We left our clothing, our furniture, and our few remaining possessions. I doubt whether my father locked the door behind him. We knew, as we exited the house that morning, that we would not return soon, if ever. We tried to comfort ourselves with the thought that we were being "relocated."

Despite the warm autumn weather, I wore a coat. We walked to the market square. German soldiers were going door-to-door, rounding up all Jews for selection and deportation. All around me was chaos, shots, screams, weeping. It was mayhem, but there was no time for fear. Adrenaline pumped through my body as we fell in line with the wave of people making their way to the market square.

Other than witnessing the hanging of the sixteen Poles in the market square, I had never seen anyone killed. I had heard gunshots since the war began, but that day, the day of the liquidation, I saw people killed right in front of me. I witnessed their killing with my own adolescent eyes. It was all happening so quickly, and it was all so arbitrary, brutal, senseless. I would become accustomed to seeing corpses and death all around me. I realized in that moment that one adapts and becomes used to things one never thought possible.

In Poland, it was common for someone to be born, be circumcised, become a bar mitzvah, have a wedding, and die – all in the same house. It was expected that people would die at home, and in Jewish homes, there were strict burial rituals to be followed in accordance with Jewish law. In the Jewish burial rituals, the body of the deceased is never left alone. The *shomrim,* the people who guard the body, recite Psalms. The Jewish Burial Society, the *Chevra Kadisha,* observes the ritual of *taharah,* the ritual purification. The body is cleansed, various prayers are recited, and the body is then wrapped in traditional burial shrouds, which are simple white linen garments. I had never witnessed this, as my paternal grandfather died when I was a baby, and all my other grandparents were then still living. So, until the hanging of the Poles in the town square, I had never seen a dead body – that is, until the day of the deportation. None of the dead lying in their homes or on the streets of my once idyllic town had the benefit of the *Chevra Kadisha,* or a proper Jewish burial.

Death itself did not frighten me as much as the process of dying. Fear was my constant companion, but hope filled my invincible heart.

When I saw bodies lying in the streets on the day of the liquidation, I knew I had two options: freeze up or decide to live. I had the courage to live. I didn't react. I pressed on, moved forward, and took one shallow breath at a time.

In many ways, we had mentally prepared for this day for three years. We could no longer turn to the leaders of the Judenrat for guidance, for they no longer wielded any power, and they too became victims of those carrying out the Aktia. The religious Jews of our town walked with the *Sh'ma,* the prayer declaring the oneness of God, on their lips, thinking that God would take care of them. Traditionally, this prayer is recited, as commanded in the bible, in the morning and evening and before sleep and also traditionally recited as one's last words before death.

It took several hours for the thousands of Jews in the ghetto to gather in the market square. Once the selection began, all those with work permits were sent to the left, the southern side of the marketplace. First, Walther Becker called out able-bodied men with work permits. After inspecting the permits, he chose strong individuals, mostly men, even some without work permits, for the group to be sent to the labor camps. My mother, father, aunt Sima, uncle Ben Zion Baranek, and I, all had work permits. Men and women were separated. My mother, not wanting to separate from her mother or her children, remained where she stood when they called out for those with permits. She refused to go voluntarily with the group that had work permits, but she was forcibly torn from us and made to stand among the group going to Tartak. My father was sent with the group going to Strelnica (*Stchelnica* in Polish), the munitions factory. My mother's sister-in-law, Bryndel, her brother Moishe Dawidowicz's wife, was standing near us. She refused to leave her young toddler. A guard grabbed the child, sending the child with the child's grandmother to the group directed to the trains, and forcing Bryndel to another group. I stood in shock at the scene unfolding before us. No one was certain where they were going, or whether they would be killed. I approached Walther Becker with my work permit. He looked at the paper, then at me, and probably thinking that I was too young, declared it a forgery and ripped it up. He chased me back to the group headed for the trains. I returned to stand with my grandmother and Chaskel, and waited anxiously.

At the end of the selection, some 1,200 men, and approximately 400 women were selected for forced labor at the Starachowice munitions factory, the Tartak woodworking factory, or the nearby Majowka camp. Those selected for work were marched out of the market square, out of the ghetto, and away from their homes for the last time. Guarded by German soldiers, they made their way on foot to their respective camps.

My Uncle Leibel, my cousin Moishe Szpagat's father, was selected for work at the munitions factory. The guards made him, and the others selected for work, run the few miles to the camps, but Uncle Leibel was weighted down with a knapsack, tripped, and lost his balance. When he fell, the Germans ordered the Ukranian guards to shoot him on the spot, in cold blood. The extent of the Germans' cruelty and viciousness, along with the other collaborators and perpetrators, was unthinkable.

The jail where my father's cousin Juzek had been imprisoned was emptied. The prisoners from the jail were loaded onto the trains first. An hour later, those remaining in the market square, mostly women, children, and the elderly, lined up in rows of five and began the miserable trek to the train station. There, people were being stuffed, one hundred or more at a time, into boxcars headed for "resettlement." We would later learn that all were sent to their almost immediate deaths at Treblinka.

I was determined. I was determined to live, and equally determined not to board that train. I looked for a way to escape, but I mentioned it to no one. I wanted to live, even if it meant sacrificing everything and everyone. I was twelve. Was I capable of making a rational decision under such circumstances? Initially I held myself back from attempting an escape because I felt responsible for Chaskel. But there was no time to think. Chaskel was only ten. Like all kids, we got along one moment and fought the next. But I loved Chaskel, as any big brother loves his little brother. The decision to walk away from my grandmother and Chaskel haunts me to this very day and will haunt me for the rest of my days, and especially my nights. If I, as the big brother, couldn't protect my little brother, and if my parents couldn't protect their children, what could anyone do? We were all on our own, each seeking to survive. Alone, I could possibly escape and hope to survive. I will never know whether Chaskel and I could have survived together. More likely than not, we would have been found and shot, but I will never know what could have been – my burden for life, my survivor's guilt.

There must have been fifty or more cattle cars lined up on the train tracks, and perhaps two passenger cars. I knew in a deep place within me, within my soul, that I was not meant to get on that train. I felt it in my gut in a visceral way.

My grandmother, Chaskel, and I walked past the central square where I had witnessed the hangings. Now the Poles were all shut up in their homes, perhaps already staking out their claims of the Jews' abandoned homes. As I neared the corner where the synagogue stood before the Germans burned it to the ground that fateful Yom Kippur a few years earlier, I knew it was the last chance to escape. It is a wonder that my grandmother, in her sixties at the time, turned to me and said, *"Antloyf, rateveh zich."* Run away, save yourself. Perhaps she sensed my agitation, my hesitation at getting into the cattle cars. Perhaps she wanted me to take my rightful place alongside those with proper work permits. Perhaps she knew that I could survive whatever came my way. I calmly gave Chaskel my water container and gently handed my coat to my grandmother to avoid calling attention to myself. I did not run. There was no time for tears or a long goodbye, I simply walked away at the last possible turn. Calmly and fearlessly, I headed down another street leading away from the train tracks. By some small miracle, the street was empty.

Where were all the guards?

I strode with a sense of purpose, walking down the familiar streets of my town, and soon found myself, as if drawn by an unknown force, standing in the home of the rabbi. I looked around and thought, *Surely they will find me here. I cannot stay.*

I fled the rabbi's house, turned the corner, and headed to Szmul Isser's bakery. The wood used to heat the bakery's ovens was stacked just outside the building, and I prepared a hiding spot. The bakery was owned by my friend, Kiva Kadysiewicz's grandfather, so I was familiar with the wood pile and knew it offered an excellent hiding place. I lay there surrounded by the chopped wood and listened to my breathing. I could hear the deportation, the crying, and the screaming. I was alone with my thoughts. Thus began the first of many small miracles that resulted in my survival. It also began my being conscious of talking to myself, encouraging myself to be strong, to move forward in spite of my fear, to keep my will to live intact. I had no voice to stand up for myself, my family, or my community, so I turned that voice inward. I recognized a force that had cleared an escape path for me at the very last possible moment before boarding the train.

Where were the German soldiers? Why weren't there guards on the street where I escaped? Where did the sense of peace come from that allowed me to walk away, rather than to run, to have the confidence to leave my grandmother and my brother, and to never look back?

If a German soldier had seen me as I confidently walked away from that terrible scene near the train station, then surely he must have mistaken me for a Pole, as I wore no *payos* and no arm band. Neither the soldiers nor the guards expected a Jew to have the *chutzpah*, the courage, to wander off from the German liquidation of a Jewish ghetto. All these thoughts ran through my mind. Listening to my breath reminded me that I was still alive and needed to do whatever it took to remain so.

I thought about my grandmother, and about Chaskel, and how they had boarded that packed train. *What would become of them? Where were those trains, those cattle cars, headed? Where would the relocation take them? Would I ever see them again?* These thoughts are the curse of surviving, the burden of a life contemplating the unknowable.

Although I did not see them that day, because there were hordes of people all around, and I felt swallowed up by the crowds that surrounded me and towered over me, I know that my mother's parents, and my cousins, Tilczia and Volf, also boarded those trains. Yes, my grandmother, Leah, had said to me, *"Run away! Save yourself!"* I had her permission and her blessing to go, but regardless of her encouragement, I would have gone. I was compelled to save myself.

The day began early, and now the ghetto had been cleared. Those selected to work had been transported to the work camps. Those selected to die were on the trains. The liquidation process began in the early hours of the day, the various groups were separated by about 2:00 p.m., and by 5:00 p.m. it was done. The Jewish population of

Wierzbnik, the life that I once knew, the little *shtetl*, was gone forever. Some sixty or seventy Jews were selected for the cleanup commando. They were responsible for digging two large graves, and for burying those who were shot and killed at the *Aktzia*. They sorted through the possessions of the Jewish community that the Germans had confiscated.

As I lay hidden by the pile of wood, my heart pounding in my chest, I knew I must wait until there was no more noise, and that I had to leave before it got too dark, so that I could find my way. I knew where the *Tartak* was, but I had never been inside. I was scared to live, to be alone, but I was more afraid to die. The time passed excruciatingly slowly. My town, the town of my parents, grandparents, and Jews for many generations had been rounded up and herded into locked cattle cars. I had witnessed the end of an entire Jewish community. No more would Yiddish be spoken in this town; no more would Hebrew be taught; no more would Jews study the Torah here, or be buried in the Jewish cemetery. No more would Shabbat candles shine in the homes of the Jewish souls who lived here; no more would the smell of freshly-baked challah fill the homes of the Jewish families here; no more would Jewish brides marry Jewish grooms in festive ceremonies under a *chuppah*, nor would Jewish babies be circumcised here. For all but the few of us who managed to survive the *Great Aktzia* on that fateful day, Wierzbnik was, as Hitler had promised, *Judenfrei*.

After the screams and shots had quieted, I emerged from the pile of wood. As I rounded the first corner, a Polish boy of about sixteen spotted me and ran after me, shouting, "You Jew! Where did you hide?" and he threatened to turn me in. I ran the mile or more to the woodworking factory known as Tartak and managed to elude the Pole who had spotted me. I didn't know whether the train holding the Jewish community of Wierzbnik had yet begun its journey to Treblinka, but for the souls on that train, wherever it was, their fate was already sealed. For others, including myself, our fates remained uncertain. But in that moment I made a firm decision: I would remain the born optimist that I was and stay the course. I was determined to forge ahead, to find a way, and hopefully to survive.

I arrived at the camp at dusk. Two dead bodies lay at the entrance of Tartak, including a young boy from Plock whom I knew from the ghetto. I learned that he and another unlucky soul were shot for failing to turn over their few remaining *zloty*. No matter how many dead bodies I saw, it was still shocking, mostly because I thought the camp was safe, but I was learning that there was no longer such a thing as *safety*. My childhood innocence was gone. I had already seen too much – and the war was just beginning.

I made my way to the back of the camp, undetected by the Ukrainian guards, and sneaked over a fence. Thus my 32-month stay in camps began, 21 of those months in Tartak. Being in a camp vital to the Nazi War effort saved the lives of many, including me, at least for a time.

As the day began, the Jewish ghetto of Wierzbnik was comprised of 5,400 souls. By the end of that terrible day 1,600, (1,200 men and 400 women) had been sent to work camps. The other 3,800 or so were sent to the killing factory known as Treblinka – a word we had never heard before, but one that we would never forget.

From the private collection of Martin Baranek.

"The German people in its whole character is not warlike, but rather soldierly, that is, while they do not want war, they are not frightened by the thoughts of it."

— Adolf Hitler, *The speeches of Adolf Hitler, April 1922-August 1939*

TARTAK LABOR CAMP

I SOON FOUND my mother, and we were relieved to see one another, but were overcome with immense sadness for the rest of our family. At first, we believed the trains were taking our family and friends to work camps, but after much time passed without any news, we understood what the silence meant and never spoke of it.

My mother had a permit to work at Tartak (as did I, before Becker ruthlessly destroyed it), and my father had his permit to work at the Strelnica munitions factory. The camps in Wierzbnik now operated with Jewish slave labor, not just forced labor. We had become the physical property of the SS and were rented out on a contractual basis to German corporations to perform work for the German war effort.

After the ghetto was emptied, crews were ordered to clean out the homes of the Jews and to assemble valuables for auctioning off to the local Poles. Anything that remained after the auction was boxed up and taken away in trucks. Soon after the Jews were eliminated from Wierzbnik, the Poles took over the abandoned property. The Germans, too, took what they wanted. Those selected for the clean-up commando remained in the ghetto before being sent to work camps.

Tartak produced ammunition crates and other wood products. Strelnica produced shell and grenade casings and other ammunition. There were no barracks at Tartak to house some three hundred Jewish workers, just a large hall for women, and another one for men, above the factory. The upstairs of the factory held rows of wooden cots separated by slats. The men's sleeping area did not have bunks. A separate structure was used as a kitchen and another had outhouses. The overcrowding and lack of indoor plumbing and running water led to sickness and disease. Men and women worked six days per week. The camp was not surrounded by barbed wire, but everyone knew the consequence of being caught outside the camp.

There were three Germans overseeing the camp: Fiedler, the head of the camp; Piatek, the manager; and a fearsome woman: Fraulen Lutz, Fiedler's secretary and lover. The Germans employed Ukrainians, Lithuanians, and Poles to run the camp.

On my second or third day, the Nazi authorities lined us up, to count the number of Jews in the camp. This was the first of many *appels* I would be required to attend. I was a scrawny youth, just twelve years old. The Sipo officer, Becker, the one who had torn up my work permit and sent me back to the group bound for the trains, grabbed me by the throat and asked, "How old are you?"

"Fifteen," I lied. "I have been working here at Tartak for three months, *Herr Hauptsturmfuehrer*," bestowing on Becker a higher rank than he had achieved, hoping to flatter him. The factory manager, Piatek, came to my rescue, and stood up to Becker, saying, "It is true. We need a small boy to clean the equipment." Piatek did not need to lie to save my life, but he showed compassion, at his personal peril. There were some fifty children at the Starachowice camps. Some had been issued work permits before the liquidation of Wierzbnik, and may have been working the night shift, the night before the *Aktzia*, sparing them the scene at the market square. Others lied about their ages, as I had. Others, who had been hiding during the liquidation, sneaked into the Starachowice camps when it became too risky to be on the outside. My friend, Kiva, had escaped the fate of the train, as did I, and made his way into Tartak, where we were reunited. I told him how I had hidden in the log pile next to his grandfather's bakery.

Kiva told me that he had escaped the market square hours before I did, hiding out until evening when he also sneaked into Tartak.

Unless the Germans came to our camp, there was no daily roll call. Our morning began with soup or bread. Then our work began. A bell rang, signaling a half-hour midday break. Sometimes we ate our meager lunches outside. We were each given a *manashke,* a bowl and a spoon, which we kept with us at all times and which were essential to our survival. Without that bowl or spoon, we could not eat our meals, often only watery soup. We stopped work in the evening. Men and women were separated at night, but I was comforted by the fact that I could always find my mother, and I saw her during the day. At night, I slept soundly alongside Kiva and the other boys and men. I had no dreams, no nightmares, just a death-dark sleep. *Tomorrow is another day,* I would tell myself to get through another night. I didn't dare question why this was happening to us, and to me.

It was noisy in the factory because of all the electric saws and machinery. I was constantly looking over my shoulder, to scan for the SS. If they came to the camp, I found a way to hide. They often entered the camp without warning. Seeing the high black leather boots of the SS reinforced my fear. There were no consequences for the SS when they tortured or killed a Jew, so we all did our best to stay out of their line of sight. We at Tartak were luckier than our brethren at Strelnica, who endured regular visits by the SS and further "selections." It did not take us long to learn what the selections meant – a random choosing of men, women, or children who would be separated and summarily murdered. Although our camp was not immune to maltreatment, or to beatings, or murder by the SS, they were less frequent events than at the neighboring camps of Strelnica and Majowka. Strelnica prisoners were subjected to more violence and selections, and the work they were forced to perform was more taxing.

Becker and his police came to Tartak occasionally. Regular selections at Strelnica were conducted by the factory security force and others in charge, including Willi Althoff, but to us they were all SS, even if they weren't actually members of that group.

Although food was by no means sufficient, we did not starve at Tartak. We depended upon the black market for additional rations. Having money or items to exchange was crucial to supplementing our diets and maintaining our strength. For those of us who were local Wierzbnikers, it was somewhat easier to access the black market. Our friend Rose Milman, (Szmul Isser's daughter) whose children were killed by Tomczyk (the policeman), had owned a bakery that was *aryanized,* taken over by a German soldier named Bastian. A baker by trade, he supplied the Germans with bread and other items. A decent man, he would sneak bread to Mrs. Milman at Tartak whenever he could. She shared it with as many of us as possible. This additional meager nourishment went a long way toward helping us remain strong.

As the two youngest workers at Tartak, Kiva (Szmul Isser's grandson) and I did not have assigned jobs, but worked as gofers, performing various tasks, including making ammunition boxes and stretchers. There were different departments at Tartak for handling wood. Trees would be felled in the forests and transported to Tartak by non-Jews. The trees would then be cut, cured, and painted. Some days, I cleaned up the sawdust. Other days I transported boxes to and from the painting department. Each day was more or less the same. We fell into a routine, working and hoping for better days ahead. At the end of the day, I fell upon my cot, dead tired. We worked constantly, were undernourished, and the stress of our situation added to our physical and mental exhaustion. I missed my house, my family, my brother, my old life. The changes and the losses were unbearable.

Live today, hope for tomorrow, try not to think of the past. I began speaking to myself, coaching myself, and willing myself to live and to survive.

The head of the camp, Fiedler, lived in a villa outside the camp. Whenver an SS member arrived at Tartak for an *Aktia,* he would get into his Mercedes and flee. It was said that he had a weak heart and couldn't take it when the Germans came into the camp to beat people, or worse. Although Fiedler did not seem to like carrying out violent actions directly, the same could not be said of his secretary and lover, Fraulein Lutz. She possessed a demonic nature, and wielded her position of power in Fiedler's absence.

At night, many local prisoners sneaked out of the camp and tried to recover some of their belongings. My mother sneaked out often, as it was easier for women like her who spoke Polish well and didn't look typically Jewish. She told me little of these risky escapes. All I knew was that she brought me food as often as she could. We had some inkling of happenings in the outside world but could only stay focused on making it through each day. While we heard rumors that the Germans were being defeated, it was difficult to hold on to any kind of lasting hope without access to radios and newspapers.

Szmul Isser, the baker and Kiva's grandfather, was a religious man. He, and everyone else in Tartak, knew how I had hidden in the log pile outside his bakery during the liquidation. No one could believe I had just walked away from the deportation. I could barely believe it myself. They all thought it miraculous. Szmul Isser; his son-in-law, Godel Kadysiewicz; and Godel's four sons, Avraham, Hillel, Eli, and Kiva, were all in Tartak. Avraham could not take the stress of all that he had witnessed, and suffered a complete break with reality. Had the Germans discovered that Avraham had lost his mind, they surely would have shot him, so everyone tried to conceal the truth. His grandfather, Szmul, resorted to tethering the boy by a rope so he could not wander off, whatever it took to help his grandson survive.

Avraham's father, Godel Kadysiewicz, was a strong and burly man, and had been a war hero in the Polish Army during World War I. In spite of having his father-in-law and his four sons in Tartak with him, Godel was like a caged animal. He needed to escape. Perhaps his experiences in World War I gave him the confidence to try. Perhaps he thought he could reach the partisans, who could help him overtake Tartak. Perhaps he just couldn't cope with losing control over his life. We will never know his thinking. One night, Godel sneaked out of Tartak and made his way into the forest. At roll call, when Becker realized Godel had escaped, he counted off every tenth person and had them line up against the wall. Avraham was selected, and was forced to stand against the wall, waiting for execution. This was common practice to keep prisoners from attempting escape. If those contemplating escape knew that many others would suffer because of their actions, they were less likely to take the risk. Another small miracle occurred: On that particular day, rather than shooting the prisoners lined up against the wall, Becker ordered everyone inside. For Avraham, the near-death experience restored his sanity. From then on, he was lucid and was able to work.

We later learned that Piatek had spoken with Becker, pleading, "What will I do for workers? These workers are essential to the war effort." Shooting every tenth prisoner would have resulted in thirty fewer laborers. There were few remaining Jews to replace those killed or transported.

A few days later, when Godel reached the Partisans in the forest, they refused to let him in. He was lucky that they didn't kill him. Out of options, Godel was forced to return to Tartak. When Becker found out about Godel's return, he beat Godel so badly that anyone else, someone without Godel's physical strength, would certainly have died from the wounds inflicted by the crazed Becker.

I had two second cousins at Tartak, Arie and Moishe Kopf. Moishe, a *meister* carpenter (a master), was married to Rivka, a shrewd woman. Early on, Rivka sensed that danger lay ahead for Poland's Jews. While Moishe was working at Tartak, during the ghetto days before the liquidation of Wierzbnik, Rivka had Moishe craft a cupboard, a wooden hiding place with no windows. In reality, the cupboard resembled a coffin. Although it seems incomprehensible, Moishe and Rivka hid their two small children, Yossi and Tzivia Kopf, in this small cupboard for nearly eighteen months. It defies all reason that these children could remain calm and quiet for long stretches of time in the dark. Sometimes, during the day, Rivka would ask me to go stay in the hiding place, to keep her children company. We remained as still as possible, whispering to one another, but even at such a young age, my cousins realized the seriousness of the situation, and did not let their hiding place be known. Although the circumstances posed a risk to all Tartak prisoners, no one let on about the children, or the hiding place.

The conditions at Tartak were bearable, even though we had all experienced trauma, and many were walking around in shock. We were tormented by bed bugs, but lucky to have no lice. When I was thirteen, there was an outbreak of typhus. I contracted it, but was able to keep it a secret. If this fact had become public knowledge, especially to Fraulen Lutz, she would certainly have sent me to my death. There was a Jewish doctor at the camp, but he could do little to aid the sick. His only medicines were alcohol, spirits, and compresses. I had a terrible fever and hallucinations, but with my mother's help and the doctor's rudimentary treatment, I soon recovered. Later on, Fraulen Lutz found out about the outbreak and phoned the SD. She ordered workers to build four stretchers and had prisoners, including Moishe Zucker a Wierzbnik lantzman, take the infirm on the stretchers to the Jewish cemetery. One of the sickly prisoners was Moishe's own son; another was Abraham Goldstein. At the cemetery, the Germans shot the four on the stretchers. The prisoners who carried them on the stretchers, including Moishe Zucker, who witnessed the killing of his own son, were forced to dig a ditch to bury the four bodies.

Thank God I was able to keep my illness a secret; thank God my mother was there to tend to me; thank God the doctor had whatever compresses he had to help break my fever.

Why am I thanking God? Where has God been all this time? Where was God when Moishe Zucker had to carry his own son to his death?

At a time in my life when I should have been preparing to

become a bar mitzvah, having turned thirteen in Tartak, I had lost all faith in God. Had the war not interrupted my life, I would have gone to the *shtiebel* with my father and grandfather, had an *aliyah* (being called to the *bimah* to read from the *Torah*), and begun using *tefillin* (prayer phylacteries), a set of small black leather boxes containing scrolls of parchment containing verses from the Torah. The boxes are attached to leather straps that one wraps around the head, arm, and hand during daily prayers, to demonstrate deference to God. The ceremony of becoming a bar mitzvah is the Jewish rite of passage from boyhood to manhood. But I did not need a ceremony to become a man. Manhood was forced upon me at age nine, when the war broke out in Poland. The war robbed me of becoming a bar mitzvah, but worse, it robbed me of my belief in God. No one should witness what I had already seen with my own two eyes at my young age – or at any age.

Working conditions in Tartak were not as difficult as those in Majowka or Strelnica, where my father and uncle worked. Those camps had furnaces to fabricate munitions. At Tartak, we merely manufactured the packaging for the munitions' transport. Our suffering was all relative. Tartak's location in southern Poland and our usefulness to the war effort gave us the advantage of being among the last camps of workers to be transported to Auschwitz, the Nazi's centralized killing center.

In the fall of 1943, my mother bribed several guards to arrange for my father's transfer from Strelnica to Tartak. My parents could now see each other, and I could remain close to my father, seeing him during the day and sleeping near him at night. It was another miracle. Being with my parents under the same roof gave me comfort and somewhat eased my fear.

I remained in Tartak from October 1942 to July 1944. We had little communication with the outside world, as the war raged on around us. Jews in labor camps and concentration camps in Germany were already being transported to Auschwitz and Majdanek when we arrived at Tartak. Jews were being transported to Auschwitz from Norway, Hungary, Greece, France, Austria, and Italy, and from cities such as Berlin, Krakow, Bialystok, and Vilna, and from camps such as Theresienstadt. Millions of Jews, Gypsies, political prisoners, Catholics, homosexuals, the physically disabled, and others targeted by the Nazis were rounded up, forced into ghettos with little or no food, stripped of their possessions, and eventually transported to one of the numerous death camps. Others were shot or succumbed to disease or starvation in the work camps.

When camps such as Belzec, Treblinka, and Sobibor were no longer used, the Nazis ordered special units of slave laborers to bury bodies in mass graves, or to dig up the bodies to burn them. Others were forced to dismantle the camps, plow them over, and plant trees in an effort to leave no trace of them. The world was awakening to the reality of Hitler's mission to annihilate the Jews, and other "undesirables," but help was slow to come.

In April 1944, prisoners arrived in Tartak from Majdanek. They confirmed the rumors of "The Final Solution" and the gassing and mass execution of Jews and other prisoners. Our false sense of security at Tartak was unravelling. Those from outside Wierzbnik had a harder time adjusting to life in the Starachowice camps because they lacked connections both in and out of the camp, and it was difficult to break into the established camp hierarchy. Still, we did not want to believe what these new arrivals were revealing to us about what was happening elsewhere in Poland. Our minds could not grasp what these prisoners were telling us.

Could they have lost their minds? How could it be true? How could civilized people murder us just because of our religion? Could they wipe us out entirely? I must live. I must not let the Germans prevail.

In retaliation for an attempted escape from Tartak in July 1944, the prisoners were separated, men from the women, and sent by trucks to the Starachowice munitions factory. When they came to take us from Tartak for the transport, a number of younger prisoners jumped from the building into the river behind the factory and made their way to the forest to the partisans. My uncle, Moishe Dawidowizc, my mother's brother, was among those who fled. Instead of running to the partisans, though, he ran to Sezaw, where my grandparents had their farm before moving to Wierzbnik, and where we fled during the German invasion of Poland. My uncle tried to hide out among the Poles. He thought he could turn to them for assistance, but we later learned from some who had fled with him that the Poles not only killed him, but beheaded him.

My father's first cousin, Moishe, his wife Rivka, and their two children hid in the coffin cupboard that he had made in anticipation of such a moment. Moishe's brother, Arieh, knocked repeatedly at the entrance, but Rivka refused to let him in. Fearing that Arieh's knocking would reveal them all, Moishe finally opened the door and the five of them remained there, undetected. We had no sense that the Russians and the Allies were gaining ground, and that the Germans had retreated from some strongholds to the east. Tartak was abandoned soon after the prisoners were sent to the munitions factory. The Kopf family stayed in the deserted Tartak factory, sneaking out at night, scavenging what they could. Remarkably they survived, and made their way to Palestine. Rivka's foresight, notably her instincts to have her husband build a coffin cupboard, ensured their survival. Who knows why some fear the worst and prepare, while others delude themselves into thinking that nothing bad could befall them?

During the chaos that ensued when the prisoners were being trucked from Tartak to the munitions factory, I lost sight of my mother and was not able to say goodbye to her. I did not know whether I would ever see her again. We stayed at the munitions factory for three nights, men separated from the women. On a Thursday we were loaded onto cattle cars, only to be unloaded and returned to the munitions factory. On Friday, July 28, 1944, we were reloaded into the cars, uncertain of the train's destination. There were 1,800 to 2,000 of us crammed into the cars, 100 to 150 per car. There was room enough only to stand, and a pot in the corner for a bathroom. My father, Uncle Ben Zion, and I were fortunate to be together in an open-air car. Guards sat atop the adjoining cars, with guns ready. The train car was similar to the enclosed cars with high wooden walls and a sliding door, just no roof. Many in the enclosed cars suffocated from the stale air, from the extreme heat, and from being packed so tightly that their lungs could not expand. At least for us in the open car, we had sufficient air to breathe.

A dozen or so prisoners from the Majdanek camp were in the first cattle car, along with the leadership of the munitions camp. These prisoners, and others, suffered at the hands of the camp hierarchy. Those prisoners from elsewhere, without status or the ability to trade on the black market, were assigned the least desirable jobs, such as working in the blast furnaces. They grew resentful of the Jewish leadership within the camp very rapidly. With their bare hands, the angry dozen from the Majdanek transport killed fourteen or fifteen members of the Jewish leadership of Starachowice. The perpetrators of this violence had sought revenge against their Jewish brethren, whom they perceived as having betrayed them at Starachowice.

Death in the cars was common, but far less common was the outright murder of fellow Jews. Among the dead in the first car were my dentist, Dr. Kurta, and Dr. Jacob Kramash. It was rumored that the doctors had committed suicide by poison, but we will never know for certain.

The predictability of life in Tartak had come to an end. We did not know what dread lay ahead for us. We thought we had experienced the worst loss and suffering we could imagine, but we would soon learn that what we had endured in the Wierzbnik Ghetto and at Tartak was nothing compared to what was forthcoming.

Yad Vashem photo archive, Jerusalem, 2600/5

"First they came for the socialists, and I did not speak out—because I was not a socialist. Then they came for the trade unionists, and I did not speak out—because I was not a trade unionist. Then they came for the Jews, and I did not speak—because I was not a Jew. Then they came for me—and there was no one left to speak for me."

— Martin Niemoller

AUSCHWITZ-BIRKENAU

WHEN THE TRAINS stopped on the tracks that first night to let other trains pass, we could hear shooting. We hoped the partisans were engaging the Germans, but we had no way of knowing what was happening on the other side of the thin wooden planks of the cattle car. We could hear additional cars being attached and added to our train in the final segment of our transfer. We struggled to make space for ourselves in the cramped car. I was comforted by the fact that I was with my father and my uncle. Once again, we moved down the tracks toward our ultimate destination. We did not know where the tracks ended or how long we would remain confined in the car with nothing to eat, nothing to drink. Day turned to night. Night turned to day. And the train rolled ever onward.

Early Sunday morning, before sunrise, the train decelerated and stopped. We saw, by looking through slats in the tiny windows, prisoners in what appeared to be striped pajamas. From my boyhood imagination, it looked to be some kind of insane asylum. We could not see signs indicating the name of the town or the station where we had arrived, but there was a platform. Suddenly, the car doors were flung open. We were met by hostile German soldiers who were holding back snarling and barking attack dogs who lunged at us as we descended from the train. The German soldiers, in response, pulled hard on the leashes to counteract the dogs' strength. Those powerful dogs were trained to attack, kill, and intimidate.

As the doors opened, the bodies of the dead leaders of the Jewish community of Starachowice tumbled out of the first car. The Germans did not know about the revenge killing taken against these former community leaders. Some thirty-six hours after leaving Starachowice, and traveling some one hundred forty miles, we had arrived at Auschwitz-Birkenau. It was a hot summer day. We were exhausted, physically and emotionally. Our legs were cramped and we were famished, having been on the train from Friday to Sunday, without food or water, and only a bucket for a toilet.

Because we were a transport of prisoners from a work camp, there were allegedly no elderly or children in our group, and selections would have presumably already taken place in Starachowice prior to our transport. We therefore faced no selection process at the arrival platforms. Perhaps too the early hour of our arrival on a Sunday helped ensure our entry into the camp without a selection. This small miracle, of not having to face a selection, again allowed me to survive. Surely a scrawny boy, shy of his fourteenth birthday, would have been sent to the left, to die in the gas chamber.

My father had concealed two gold coins in his pocket. Each American five-dollar gold coin was worth about one hundred dollars at the time, a great deal of money. He gave one to his friend, Godel, Kiva's father, to hold under his tongue. He hid one in his own mouth. The men were taking a huge risk. Truly, their lives were at stake, for anyone caught attempting to bring anything into the camp would have been shot. My father had to take a chance though; anything of value could be used in exchange for food, or for a better work assignment. We were two fathers and two sons. Kiva and I had already become like brothers from our time at Tartak, looking out for one another, but now at Auschwitz we would need to rely upon each other even more. Our survival depended on it.

We were disoriented upon arrival: exhausted, hungry, thirsty, frightened. Guards beat us as we exited the train, and they forced us to march to the barracks to be processed. First the guards ordered us to undress. Then they commanded us to have our heads shaved. Next they ordered us to the showers. We had heard rumors, and were frightened as they forced us into the shower room. We were thankful when water sprayed from the showerheads, and not gas. After the shower, we were doused with DDT to prevent the spread of lice. The poison burned our skin, but we were thankful to be alive, for having survived the train journey. They gave each of us a uniform that resembled the striped pajamas that we saw being worn by the other prisoners: pants, a shirt, and a cap. We kept our essential *manashke* and spoon with us, brought from Tartak.

Stay sharp and keep your wits about you. My number one goal is to stay alive by not standing out, not getting caught, being smart, appearing older than I am, and not losing hope.

At Tartak, we wore our own clothes. Now we were forced to wear a uniform, likely already worn by someone whose ashes had since floated skyward through the chimneys from which smoke seemed to emanate ceaselessly. Upon arrival at Auschwitz-Birkenau, we knew that everything here would be different – harder, scarier, riskier. We had heard whispers about Auschwitz and Birkenau and the dreaded gas chambers. We could see them now with our own eyes, not only the chimneys but the ashes as well. We could see the spirals of ashes ascending towards heaven. Ashes to ashes, I thought, dust to dust, but this was not how it was intended. We could no longer delude ourselves about "rumors."

When I registered at Auschwitz, I gave my birth year as 1928 in order to make myself older.

Certainly a teenager of sixteen years would be more desirable and fit to work than a mere boy of fourteen.

Some boys from the Starachowice camps were somehow able to stay with their mothers, but I remained with my father and uncle in the men's camp, where work was more brutal and selections more frequent.

My father, my uncle Ben Zion, and I were together when we received our tattoos, so our numbers were sequential: My uncle's was A18804, mine was A18805 and my father's was A18806. Ali Rosenberg, also a prisoner, tattooed our numbers on our left arms, as was done with all the prisoners at Auschwitz-Birkenau. I peered into his face as he scratched out the tattoo on my arm. Ali dipped a needle into the ink before pricking it into our flesh. The needle stung, but we had learned to endure pain without wincing. The tattoo was but one more act to dehumanize the Jews and the other prisoners. We became mere numbers, interchangeable, fungible, like livestock. The circumstance of our sequential numbers would prove helpful to me in the future. After the tattooing, we were no longer called by our names, only by our numbers. We were nothing more than a commodity to the Germans. Only prisoners of Auschwitz were tattooed with numbers. Prisoners from Majdanek had tattoos with the letters "KL" (*koncentracion lager*) meaning concentration camp, but they did not have tattooed numbers.

After a day of intake at Auschwitz-Birkenau, on August 2, 1944, the guards ordered us to "C Camp" (the Gypsy camp), where we were assigned to our bunks for the night. The chimneys of the gas chambers were in direct view of the barrack. We heard a lot of commotion outside but did not know what was going on. That night some 3,000 Gypsies were gassed and their bodies were burned. I could smell the burning flesh all throughout the night. It was a nauseating, unforgettable smell that coated the inside of my nose and throat. The Gypsies were taken away to make room for our transport. They had outlived their usefulness for the Germans, and now, with our arrival, we would replace the weak.

Would we meet the same fate as the Gypsies? How much time did we have before they replaced us with another recently arrived transport? How could human beings be so barbaric? How do the perpetrators of these atrocities go home at night and have normal interactions with family and friends, knowing what they had done? What has happened to the collective conscience of these people? These were questions of mine, then and now.

The next morning, we experienced our first of many prisoner *appels,* (roll calls), at Auschwitz-Birkenau. We were assigned jobs based upon individual skills and the Germans' needs. My father was sent to Buna (Monowitz), also known as Auschwitz III, a camp that housed rubber factories. Very few survived Buna. When my father was selected, we did not expect to see him again. At thirty-nine years old, he had lost his youngest son, been separated from his wife, lost his home, his business, all his possessions, his freedom, and his dignity. Before he was sent away, my father handed me the gold coin that he had sneaked into this wretched place. I was to share it with Kiva, if necessary. He was a fair man, and sharing the coin with Kiva was my father's way of thanking Godel for risking his own life to also smuggle one of the gold coins into the camp. We were all in this together, and we did what we could to look out for one another – our friends, our family, our community.

There was little time for a proper goodbye. I hoped to see my father again, and the thought of being reunited with my family at some future date helped me cope. I couldn't be sure though. It had been so long without news from anyone from our town who was on that ill-fated train the day of the liquidation, and I knew deep inside me that those souls were already gone from this world. I did not want to acknowledge that explicitly, but that thought remained lodged somewhere in my subconscious. So when my father was separated from us and sent to Buna, I swore to keep him always in my heart and to find a glint of optimism deep inside myself.

My uncle was selected for Commando, a fairly desirable job. Kiva and I were among the youngest in camp and initially were not given jobs. C Camp was mostly a transfer camp. Trains arrived at night; men were brought to C Camp where there was a selection process. The strong were sent to labor in one of the forty Auschwitz sub-camps. Those the Nazis deemed unfit for work were sent to their deaths.

The summer of 1944 was a particularly treacherous time to be a prisoner at Auschwitz-Birkenau. The Nazi killings escalated to a record 9,000 per day, a rate exceeding the capacity of the crematoria. Slave laborers were forced to dig six huge pits around the area of the crematoria to accommodate the large number of bodies. The charred bodies and ashes remain buried in the mass graves.

Only later we would come to learn that while the killings at Auschwitz-Birkenau were being stepped up, Russian troops had liberated a Nazi concentration camp in Poland in July of 1944. The camp, Majdanek, was just four kilometers from the city center of Lublin, not located in a remote forest where atrocities were easily hidden, as at Treblinka and Auschwitz. We had met some former prisoners of Majdanek when they arrived in Starachowice. They had already seen firsthand what the death camps were like. They were the prisoners who had verified the truth of the gas chambers and reported what was really happening in concentration camps and killing centers. To them, the labor camps in Starachowice must have been a welcome improvement. Despite beatings, and some selections, at least there were no gas chambers. Majdanek, originally a POW camp, was visible from the main road and was surrounded by small villages. Thousands perished at Majdanek, many from the Lublin region, as well as from Warsaw. The Nazis celebrated *Aktion Erntefest* ("Operation Harvest Festival") in November 1943, when they massacred some 42,000 prisoners. This atrocity included the infamous machine gunning of 18,000 Jews in one day at Majdanek camp itself. The Germans forced the prisoners to dig ditches, and to line up, one hundred to a row, to be gunned down. The next hundred were forced to lie down on the fresh corpses for their turn to be killed. This continued from morning to night, line after line of one hundred people at a time. Classical music blared from speakers, so that the neighboring townspeople would not hear the gunfire or the victims' screams. The other 24,000 victims were killed at other camps in the Lublin district, for example at Poniatowa and Trawniki, where the dead were actually burned on open grills, not in crematoria with smoke stacks. Surely, the citizens must have suspected something sinister was occurring. Surely the townspeople saw that thousands entered the gates at Majdanek, yet none emerged. The smoke stacks were visible for all to see, and the endless chain of smoke that emanated from those stacks would certainly have spread the unmistakable scent of burning flesh. It was said that ash fell on the city for at least a week after the *Aktion Erntefest*. None could feign ignorance of the massacres occurring all around them.

Auschwitz-Birkenau was unlike Majdanek, as Auschwitz-Birkenau was more secluded, despite its massive scale. Oswiecim, the town from which Auschwitz takes its name, along with many surrounding villages, were razed and the inhabitants forced to relocate before Auschwitz-Birkenau began to be used as a labor and death camp. Birkenau, known as Auschwitz II, was a death camp of 175 acres. The camp, originally designed to house 125,000 prisoners, was expanded to a capacity of 200,000. Toward the end of the war, it was used as a camp to assemble prisoners together before they were transferred to labor camps, as the Germans were struggling to stave off Allied forces closing in on them. Although there were prisoners of war from the Soviet Union and from other countries who perished in Auschwitz's complex of sub-camps, the overwhelming majority of all victims died in Birkenau. We were living in a cemetery, but soon we too could be among the buried, burned, and forgotten.

We were constantly surrounded by death at Auschwitz-Birkenau, but saw many contradictions within the Nazi process. The Germans venerated classical music. Many of Europe's most accomplished Jewish musicians and artists wound up in Auschwitz, destined for extermination. Birkenau's orchestra comprised some of Europe's finest musicians, who were forced to play for the prisoners as they exited the camp in the morning and returned in the evening. The musicians had their own barracks, and in the beginning, before we had jobs, Kiva and I would listen to their daily practice. By stealing ourselves away in the musicians' barracks, we kept ourselves occupied and out of sight of the German guards. One had to stay useful in

Auschwitz-Birkenau; otherwise, the gas chambers awaited. Without assigned jobs, we did what we could to stay undetected. Sometimes that meant hiding in the barrack playing cards; other times it was listening to the musicians rehearse.

We remained in C Camp barracks from our arrival in July until October. I was like a tiger in a cage, restless. No one could be trusted, not even those in one's own barrack. It was important to have a buddy, and I had Kiva. We looked after one another. In many ways, our lives were parallel. We shared so much and seemed to have comparable good luck. We were childhood friends who had each escaped the liquidation of the Wierzbnik Ghetto, and now we had survived Tartak and the transport to Auschwitz-Birkenau. We were bonded as few human beings are in life.

During the summer of 1944, the Lodz ghetto was liquidated, and 60,000 Jews were transported to Birkenau. Others were sent from the Lodz ghetto to Chelmno. Lodz was the last remaining Jewish ghetto in Poland. Time was running out for the Jews, as Hitler's "Final Solution" accelerated. The Third Reich had gained power and territory, and it seemed that the Russians, English, and Americans might not advance in time to save those of us who remained. We had very little news from the outside world, but rumors swirled within the camp. One of the last transports carrying Hungarians also arrived in late summer 1944.

Does anyone know we are here? Does anyone care? Why don't the Allies bomb the train lines so the transports to the camps can stop? Will we be saved in time? Do not give up hope, do not give up hope, do not give up. My inner dialogue was filled with questions and, always, with mantras of hope and survival.

Sundays were special. There was no work, and we were sometimes given pea soup and bologna. We tested the soup's quality by sticking our spoons upright in the bowl. If the spoon fell over, the soup was mostly liquid, but if the spoon stood straight up, there was more substance to it. We savored every bite of the disgusting nutrition. Food was brought to our barracks in big pots carried by prisoners. This method of distribution reduced the risk of someone sneaking in line for more than one portion.

The Nazis thought of everything.

Each prisoner had a *manashke*, a small container for food. We guarded the *manashke* as a precious possession. Without it, one could not eat the meager portions of soup allotted us. I had learned the value of my *manashke* at Tartak. Sometimes, when we saw the prisoners transporting the big vats of soup, we would run by and dunk our *manashkes* into the deep pot to make off with an extra portion. One time I was caught doing this and the beating I received dissuaded me from trying that again. The *kapo* who caught me tossed me headfirst into a barrel and beat me severely, giving me ten blows with his cane. The consequences for our crimes were always disproportionate, and the *kapos* were often as cruel as the Nazis themselves.

Even on Sundays, our brief break from grueling work, the prisoners' minds were still working, and there was always the threat of a selection or killing. We thought about our lives before the war, about the loss, and pain, and suffering. Without work or a way to keep our hands busy, we focused more on our hunger and exhaustion. Many hurled themselves against the electrified fences to end their misery. I recall more of these suicides occurring on Sundays.

Do not think about life before the war, do not think about life in Wierzbnik, and do not think of the past. Think only of the present, live for this moment, live for this day, and just continue to live.

Kiva and I spent a lot of time playing cards. We especially liked the game "1000," similar to gin rummy. We were just two young teenagers who never imagined, as young boys in our wonderful town of Wierzbnik, that our lives would be upended so violently and so completely.

On *Rosh Hashanah* 1944, during the afternoon *appel,* there was a selection. Kiva and I were among the group of mostly younger or weaker prisoners sent to the quarantine barracks. The quarantine barrack was a holding pen for those destined for the gas chambers. The Nazis especially liked to torment Jewish prisoners by making human sacrifices on Jewish holidays. There were 300 to 400 prisoners in the barracks. The religious, and even those less so, began praying. Some were reciting *vidui*, the confessional prayers. I recognized two men in their forties, acquaintances of my father, and overheard one saying, *"See what they are doing here, what they are doing to us? Nobody will ever know what became of us. No one will ever even know that we were here."* But I know, and all the other survivors know, what became of them, and what became of millions of others who suffered and perished at the hands of the Nazis. Each survivor's life is a testament to that knowledge.

Moments away from certain *death*, I only thought of *living* as the prisoners were being led from the barracks. Kiva and I had paid attention to the changing of the guards, and when the time was right, I knew that again, like during the procession toward the trains in Wierzbnik, that I had to take my chances and plan my escape. As I stood at the threshold of the barrack, I looked left and then right, and realized, by some miracle, that there were no guards around. Like the day of the *Aktzia* in Wierzbnik when I walked away from the train, an invisible hand guided me as I ran into a neighboring barrack. Kiva, too, ran out at the same moment.

Run fast and hide.

My heart pounded as I slid my emaciated body feet-first onto my stomach and into, as luck would have it, a tiny heating oven. From inside, I closed the door of the oven with one finger. Auschwitz had been a Polish Army base before the war, so the barracks were equipped with ovens to heat the barracks in winter. (Of course, the ovens were not used to heat the barracks for us. In the barracks, we relied solely on each other's body heat, which, as emaciated as we were, provided little warmth.)

Now, inside this tiny space, I contorted my body. I could hear other prisoners being taken away. People were crying and screaming.

Where was Kiva? Had he found a place to hide in time? I hope he stays with me and that he does not go with the other unlucky souls to the gas chamber.

Please let Kiva survive...

I remained still, listening to the pounding of my heart, trying to slow and steady my breath.

Thank God I was able to hide, to cheat death again. So close, so close to death. God? Why was I thanking God? No! I don't believe in God. There is no God here in this camp. I am thankful, and I am grateful for life, but I cannot thank God for this miracle. It is just a miracle. But can there be miracles without God? It is so confusing. No, the God I grew up with could never let this happen to my family, to me, to the Jews, to human beings. There cannot be a God in heaven.

When the screaming and crying stopped, and thinking that no one was there, I let myself out. I was confronted by an incredulous Polish kapo who watched me emerge from the tiny oven.

He grabbed me by the ear. "Where did you hide?" he questioned.

I cried, begging him that I should live. I could not remember the last time I had cried, but now a stream of tears shed easily. I showed him the tiny oven where I had hidden. He let me go, and I returned to my previous barrack. With all the odds against him, Kiva, who had run in the opposite direction from me, had thankfully also found a hiding place, and now we were reunited. We had cheated death again, and now we managed to blend in with a new group of prisoners.

I sought out my uncle and gave him the gold coin my father had entrusted to me. I sensed that time was running out for us. Like the Gypsies, perhaps it was time to clear out the old, and replace us with the newly arrived. I asked my uncle to exchange the coin for smaller currency. A functioning black market operated within the camp, an example of human beings' desperate ability to procure the most basic of human necessities: food, water, clothing. We were all in survival mode, doing things not imaginable in times of peace. We were not proud of those acts such as stealing, but did what we had to do to survive. Those who worked in the kitchen had the best jobs in the camp. They often sold extra rations for money, which they used to buy themselves new shoes or a blanket, or some small creature comfort to help them stay dry, warm, strong.

The following week, on *Yom Kippur*, the Jewish Day of Atonement, Kiva and I decided to observe the ritual fast. We did this from a sense of tradition and respect for our families, less from a religious bent, or from a belief in God. Of course, we saved our daily meager portions of bread to eat after the holiday. We certainly had no intent to give up our rations altogether.

Once again, the Nazis intended to kill more Jews on a sacred Jewish day. This time, the youngest prisoners were targeted. Those from my barrack were sent to a selection conducted by the infamous Dr. Mengele. Mengele set up a measurement system for selection in front of the latrines. The measurement was one meter fifty centimeters (approximately 59 inches). Kiva and I were small and would not have passed the selection. We returned to the barrack to hide out. At roll call, we each took a pail, turned them over, and stood on them to make ourselves appear taller. A guard discovered us standing on the overturned pails. He took us by the shirt collars and sent us to the quarantine barrack, scheduled for liquidation. Again, this occurred on another sacred Jewish holiday. Kiva and I found ourselves in a quarantine barrack waiting to be sent to the gas chamber. I climbed up to the top bunk. Kiva and I changed our minds about the *Yom Kippur* fast. We were in the quarantine barrack and slated for the gas chamber, so where was the logic in holding on to a paltry ration of bread?

The portions were so poorly made that we held the pieces with two hands, or else the bread would simply fall to crumbs as we devoured it.

We saw nowhere to hide and no route of escape. Time was running out. The Germans intended to take us to the gas chambers before the gates of repentance closed, marking the end of *Yom Kippur*.

I started to feel it, that familiar pang, like hunger. Fear gripped my belly. It rose up and spread throughout my body until an electric pulse coursed through my veins. Time slowed and my senses were on high alert. The fear energized, yet exhausted me, and even though I was afraid to sleep, my eyes closed and I was in absolute darkness. I slept, but did not dream, nor did nightmares disturb my deep slumber.

I don't know how long I slept, but when I awoke the fear that was abated during my deep slumber returned at once. I felt devastated, utterly abandoned when I looked around and realized that Kiva was gone. I was startled to realize Kiva had sneaked out onto the roof and must have hidden in another barrack, leaving me alone and to my own fate. Perhaps Kiva feared our capture if caught together. Perhaps this was his moment of selfish truth – his moment to save himself, with no thought of anyone else. My thoughts turned to Chaskel. We all had to make choices, and our circumstances made our choosing painful and final. I too had made decisions to save myself, without regard to anyone else. Although we depended upon others, and took comfort in having someone to look out for us, we were all, in fact, on our own, seeking survival. Sometimes there is not safety in numbers. Sometimes there is only safety in looking after oneself.

When my uncle learned I was in the quarantine barracks and would be sent to the gas chambers, he went to the *kapo,* Yignatz, to plead for my life. My uncle had been unable to exchange the coin for smaller amounts, so he offered the *kapo* the gold coin itself. The *kapo* wanted more, but accepted what my uncle had to give. The gold coin my father had bravely hidden, worth about one hundred dollars, would go a long way on the black market, and would serve the *kapo* well.

Thank you, father, for your bravery, and for your thoughtfulness. Thank you for saving my life...

Minutes before the barracks were to be emptied, and prisoners taken to the gas chambers, the *kapo,* Yignatz, entered and called out

"Michael Baranek." Many claimed to be "Baranek," but my uncle, whose tattooed number was in sequence with mine, had wisely given the *kapo* my number, to ensure that the right person would be saved. *Kapo* Yignatz whisked me from the quarantine barrack with not three minutes to spare before the trucks backed up, taking those souls to their deaths in the nearby gas chambers. He took me back to his barrack, where I was again reunited with Kiva. I was happy to see that again my friend and I had both survived, but we both knew the truth, that Kiva had left me sleeping while he found a way to escape.

Yom Kippur – the Day of Atonement. But what did we Jewish children have to atone? What were our sins? We had been born to Jewish parents, and for this, Nazis wanted to kill us? Would the perpetrators ever seek atonement? My second escape from the gas chambers – another miracle.

A month later, on October 7, 1944, around the holiday of *Sukkot,* we saw prisoners being sent to the gas chambers. My heart hardened. I was thankful that it was they, and not I, going to certain death. After a short while, however, those condemned souls returned to the barracks.

This is unbelievable. Prisoners sent to the gas chambers never return alive. What is going on?

A revolt had occurred at the gas chamber. Three young women had smuggled dynamite into the camp and had given it to the *Sondercommando.* The *Sondercommando* transported the endless number of corpses from the gas chamber to the crematorium. The morale of this group was, understandably, among the lowest of any camp prisoners. They were in the unenviable position of having their job depend upon having other prisoners gassed. These units were replaced every two to three months, in part to prevent the survival of any eyewitnesses of the Nazi's horrific actions. This *Sondercommando* was able to use the dynamite to explode Crematorium Number Four. The three brave young women were found out and were hanged. But as a result of the explosion and the looming end of the war, the Germans stopped using the gas chambers in Birkenau in the late autumn of 1944.

Finally, there came an end to the stream of black smoke pouring forth from the chimneys, carrying ashes of the victims into the Polish sky.

That same month, we were transferred to D Camp, a more secure camp than C Camp. Selections were conducted in C Camp before the transfer. Kiva and I were selected for work in the *"Shisse Commando."* We tried to stay busy and out of sight. We assisted in unloading arriving prisoners' personal belongings and sorting them. These prisoners were destined for the gas chambers. Kiva and I were ordered to pull carts, picking up and delivering items throughout the camp. We tied a rope around our bodies to help pull the heavy carts. Our boss was a German political prisoner, a fairly decent man. Each day, he would specify where Kiva and I would go. We gathered clothes on some days, and wood on other days, for transport. Our access to the baggage confiscated from the arriving prisoners allowed us to pocket small things for ourselves, or items that could be sold or traded on the black market, such as socks or gloves. This small pilfering helped us to gain an advantage, to have some comfort or to elude death for a while longer. With each passing day of 1944, we were all closer to freedom, a fact not known to us. I could not allow myself to dream of freedom. I needed to remain focused upon the incremental task of surviving – for one more morning, one more afternoon, one more night – for one more hour.

Although prisoner morale improved after the gassing stopped at the end of October 1944, prisoners were still abused, beaten, and intimidated, and we were constantly hungry. *Kapos* walked around with canes and beat people indiscriminately. Killing continued, but on a smaller scale.

Some of the kapos were fellow Jews. How could they treat their brethren this way? Were they evil, or simply hardened by this terrible experience? Were they themselves just trying to survive?

In November 1944, in a desperate attempt to erase evidence of Nazi crimes, Himmler ordered the destruction of the crematoria at

Auschwitz. Although they had been shut down, the crematoria served as a reminder of the inhumane acts that had occurred there.

I remained at Auschwitz-Birkenau from the end of July 1944 until January 18, 1945. Times were getting tougher as the months and years of the war trudged on. Auschwitz-Birkenau was worse than Tartak, and Tartak was worse than the Wierzbnik Ghetto. I didn't allow myself to imagine how things could possibly get any worse, but soon I learned what misery and depravity awaited me.

Yad Vashem photo archive, Jerusalem, 20B03

"Never shall I forget the little faces of the children, whose bodies turned into wreaths of smoke beneath a silent blue sky."

— Elie Wiesel

THE DEATH MARCH

THE DEATH MARCH, euphemistically referred to as an "evacuation" by the Nazis, began on January 18, 1945. It would prove to be the beginning of yet the cruelest part of my war experiences. It never occurred to me to hide out in Auschwitz-Birkenau as some prisoners did. I was swept up in the mass of humanity following orders by the Germans to march.

The death march actually comprised a series of marches toward the end of World War II, from fall 1944 until April 1945. As the Russians advanced on the Eastern Front, thousands of prisoners from Nazi concentration camps outside Germany were forced to march long distances, with little or no food or water, into Germany proper and not just German territory. Thousands died of exposure, exhaustion, and dehydration. Those too weak to walk any further were executed, shot on site, their corpses littering the roadside. I was only one of 60,000 prisoners on the death march that began on January 18, 1945, from Auschwitz-Birkenau to destinations unknown to us. The intended destination, I later learned, may have been Wodzislaw ("Loslau" in German), thirty-five miles away, where prisoners were to be put on trains and sent to other camps. I was weak and disoriented and operating on little information from the outside world, a world to which I no longer belonged, and to which I had not belonged for years. I had forgotten what it was like to live a normal life. My reality had become so abnormal that I no longer knew what normal was.

It is estimated that 15,000 prisoners, out of 60,000 who left from Auschwitz-Birkenau on foot at the end of January, died along the way. Of the estimated 750,000 prisoners sent on death marches in the final weeks of the war, from numerous camps, the Germans murdered some 250,000 to 375,000. Many more died of exhaustion, starvation, and thirst. Still more simply froze to death. Thousands of bodies were heaped upon the sides of the roads as we marchers dragged ourselves on, trying to avoid that same fate.

Doors of the barracks burst open and a pile of shoes were hastily thrown into the barrack for the prisoners. I found what I thought would be a good pair, but the shoes rubbed against my thin feet. Prisoners were lined up outside, five in a row, arms linked. The Germans gave us things to carry. Of course, we also carried our *menashkas* and spoons. The orders were simple: "March." Kiva and I stayed close together. It was easy to get lost among the throngs of prisoners pushing and shoving. I remained in that oppressively dark tunnel, not knowing whether any light of freedom would appear soon, but I was hopeful that leaving Auschwitz-Birkenau would portend good things to come. It was the first time I had been outside the gates of Birkenau in six months. We had no idea where we were headed, nor for how long we would be walking. It was terribly cold – the dead of winter in Poland. We were malnourished and scantily clad in our threadbare uniforms. The uncertainty made our journey even more difficult, more terrifying. As we walked and walked, one foot in front of the other, following the columns in front of us, we would alternate positions. The three men in the middle would rest, and two on the ends remain upright, supporting those in the middle. I would rest, leaning upon my neighbors when possible. My legs kept moving forward even if my mind fell away in a stupor. I tried hard to avoid being on an end, to stay out of the German guards' sight, but we continued taking turns, physically supporting each other as best we could. Often, I imagined I was sleepwalking, delirious from the cold, the hunger, the pain in my feet. We were all but walking corpses.

That first night of the march, we slept on the snow banks. Although I was literally freezing, exhaustion overcame me, and I slept. The Germans withheld any food or water from us. The second day, anyone unable to get up or to continue marching was shot.

Keep going, keep marching. Try to ignore the pain of each step when the blisters rub against the inside of the shoes. Remember a time when you were warm and not hungry. I can do it. I've come this far. Keep going, keep marching. Keep living. One, two, three; one, two, three; one foot in front of the other.

By the third night, we had reached German territory. My feet were afire, despite the freezing temperatures of winter, and I began to falter.

"Kiva, I cannot go any further. We have no food, no water, no comfortable shoes, no warm clothes. I have no more strength. I don't know how much further they will make us walk, perhaps until we all die."

"I will carry you," responded Kiva.

"Kiva, my companion, I cannot allow you to carry me. You haven't the strength to do so. Anyway, the Germans will shoot us both if they see that we are faltering. Go on. Save yourself. Keep going. I will take my chances, but I cannot go on. My feet are aching. They are bleeding. I am wounded, my friend. You go on."

Kiva's offer to physically carry me, restored me spiritually. His words sustained me, touched me to the core. *How could Kiva think he could really carry me? We were freezing, hungry, tired, broken, but the mere act of telling me that he would carry me, knowing that if I stayed behind probably meant certain death, helped me keep my thoughts of hope even when the situation was hopeless. That simple act proved Kiva's character and helped me maintain my faith in humanity, and gave me strength and courage to soldier on.*

But when I fell behind, Kiva continued forward until I could no longer distinguish him from the others who comprised the slow wave of near-corpses. For the first time since the outbreak of the war, since Wierzbnik, since Tartak, the transport to Auschwitz-Birkenau, since all the near-misses we had encountered separately and together, I found myself alone, separated from the one person I had always counted on to be there for me, but I had no time to contemplate our parting. Kiva, my friend, my companion, my family, continued on without me. When his image slipped away and I could see him no longer, I felt vulnerable. I was unsure how I could continue on without my dear Kiva. My footing was unsteady, and I felt myself dragging and slowing down until I was making little forward progress.

I lagged behind with two to three hundred others. We slept again under the stars, open to the elements. I let some freezing snow melt on my tongue. I was nearly lifeless but somehow slept. The next morning, I expected that the Germans would shoot those of us who were too weak to continue marching, but rather than being shot, we were put together in a camp about two or three kilometers up the road. There, to my great surprise, I found Zvi Unger from my hometown of Wierzbnik. He was older than me by two years. It was comforting to find a familiar face, a friend, especially as I no longer had Kiva to watch out for me. We stayed at that camp for another day. When they lined us up for roll call, we could see the Germans setting up machine guns.

I turned to Zvi and said, "Soon as they start shooting, fall down and lay still. Pretend that you are dead." It was close to the truth. We were walking corpses by then, each rib protruding from our chests. We were weak, cold, exhausted. We were starving. When we could, we grabbed a handful of snow to quench our thirst, to try keeping our hunger at bay. There is no explaining why or how some of us were still alive. Only our spirit, our *neshamah,* propped up our physical beings. We waited. The anticipation was excruciating.

Had I survived all these months to die here on the side of this hill? I want so much to live, but perhaps the dead have it easier. At least there would be no more pain, no more hunger, no more cold. Perhaps my soul, once released from my body, would feel nothing and I would finally be free.

We stood, waiting for the bullets to pelt us, tearing through our skin. We waited for the loud bursts of gunfire, but to our great astonishment, the Germans began taking down the machine guns.

What was happening? They weren't going to kill us after all? Were the Germans saving the bullets for the advancing Russian and Allied armies? Were they running low on ammunition? Was it somehow more horrible, leaving evidence of demonic crimes on German soil, rather than in Poland, where the Germans could blame others?

Whatever the reason for this miracle, and even though our physical suffering was prolonged, we were thankful that we could live yet one more day. We were ordered into the barracks. The next day, we were loaded onto cattle cars. Another train. The hypnotic sound of the wheels turning over and over soothed me. Finally, I could rest and my feet could begin to heal. We passed through Czechoslovakia. When we slowed down or stopped, some charitable townspeople, who may have been Czech, gave us food and water – whatever they could. They passed what they could through the slats and through tiny windows that barely let in any light. The inhospitable train car was damp and cold, but this welcomed gesture of compassion from civilians boosted our spirits. Perhaps those civilians saw that the war was coming to an end and realized that things were changing – that the victims of the war might survive to tell their horror stories to the world, and those who had participated in the horror, or even just those bystanders, did not want to be judged harshly.

At one point, the train halted between two military trains. We heard planes flying low overhead. Someone said they were Russian planes. Suddenly they began shooting. Whether they realized there were cars full of prisoners is unknown, but we starving prisoners would have happily sacrificed ourselves for the sake of killing any of the German military or Nazis on the other trains. I heard ringing in my ears, and the next thing I knew, the roof had been blown off the car in which we were imprisoned, causing the doors to fall off. All the prisoners ran from the train. Some were shot and killed as they tried to get away and hide. As weak as I was, I ran as fast as my sore feet could carry me.

Run away. Save yourself. The words of my grandmother still urged me on. But where would I go? Who would help a poor Jewish prisoner like me? I was still wearing my tattered prisoner uniform. I could not count on the kindness of strangers to feed me, to clothe me, to shelter me.

After the planes flew away, shockingly, amazingly, inexplicably, we defeated prisoners sheepishly returned to the trains. We had been psychologically beaten down. We were scared and scarred. We wore prison garb. Our feet were sore and frostbitten. Who would have helped us? What fate lay beyond the trees for us? We were likely to be killed if we continued on; we were just as likely to be killed if we returned to the trains. Yet, we returned to the trains, seeing them not as a refuge, but because the uncertainty of the woods and what lay beyond.

Had I known that the end of the war was near, or had an inkling of the horror that awaited me, I would have hidden myself, or found a way to stay at Auschwitz-Birkenau. I had no information of the outside world, no way to know when walking through those gates in those terrible wooden shoes that the Russians were to liberate the camp merely nine days later. On January 27, 1945, the Russians entered Auschwitz-Birkenau and freed those who had taken their chances and hidden in the evacuated camp.

"If there is a god, he will have to beg for my forgiveness."

— Anonymously carved into the wall of Cell Block 20, Mauthuasen-Gusen Concentration Camp

MAUTHAUSEN

THE TRAIN STOPPED and we emerged from the closed cattle cars in Mauthausen near Linz, Austria, the birthplace of Adolph Hitler. This camp held not only Jewish prisoners, but Italian, French, Yugoslav, Polish, Russian, Spanish political prisoners, and Gypsies. Immediately, I felt a sense of dread. Back when I arrived at Auschwitz-Birkenau, we did not undergo a selection, but now I doubted whether my luck would be repeated.

Mauthausen itself was divided into Camp II, Camp III, and the Tent Camp. There were many sub-camps and work camps such as Gusen I, Gusen II, and Ebensee, located some thirty miles away. The Nazis used Ukrainians and others to staff the various camps, but in this prison, the guards, (the *kapos*) were psychopaths, criminals, and murderers.

In Tartak, we had worked hard and dreaded inspections by German officers, but we did not fear the gas chambers. In Auschwitz-Birkenau, we had feared the gas chambers, but knew we had a black market and could manipulate certain *kapos*. After the Nazis stopped using the gas chambers, there was, of course, an enormous sense of relief. But Mauthausen was unlike anywhere else, a place of physical and mental torture and abuse beyond our imaginations. The camp was surrounded by high walls with electrified barbed wires. We gathered in an open square, and were then sent to the showers. I moved forward, step by step, my body inching toward the shower house, my mind unable to process the circumstances. My constant companion, fear, was with me, but my legs kept carrying me toward the shower house.

We entered the showers and stood there, naked and afraid.

Is this it? Is this the end? Will it be painful? When death comes, let it be quick. I cannot endure any further suffering.

From overhead, hot water flowed out, hitting our nearly frozen skin. After the shower, there was another roll call. The Nazis were always counting us, making lists.

Why do they care about keeping lists? Once they kill us all, what will a list matter? Why do they keep counting us? Our numbers continue to subtract. Why document such details?

We stood outside for hours in the freezing cold, wet and naked, except for the wooden shoes we had been given. We stood there totally exposed to the elements. There were many times when I had feared for my life before, but this camp proved to be the true test of my fortitude. For the first time, I doubted my ability to survive. At this point, I expected to die. It was only a matter of when.

Each day was worse than the one before. I was disillusioned and without hope, and I accepted that I would not live much longer. I had seen it all too often in the camps before. Hope could feed the body, and could reassure the soul beyond what one thought humanly possible, but once hope was gone, despair attracted the angel of death.

The German guards of Mauthausen registered our transport on January 30, 1945, and assigned to me prisoner number 123586. This time, the number was not permanently etched into my arm, as it was in Auschwitz. They gave us each a pair of striped prisoner uniforms, before directing some to various sections within the camp or sending others to nearby sub-camps.

They sent me to Camp III with Zvi Unger. Thankfully I had a familiar face with me, someone who knew me from Wierzbnik, knew the kind of life I had before these terrible circumstances befell us.

Even to other prisoners, we were sometimes regarded as sub-human, but with those who knew each other from a hometown or village, we could be seen as human beings, as individuals. I was grateful to have met up with Zvi on the death march. Camp III was for those considered unfit to work. Perhaps I appeared too young and too weak to be of value. A small boy needed in the woodworking factory in Tartak was not needed here in Mauthausen, where prisoners were forced to carry granite boulders up treacherous stairs. I met up with my cousin, Moishe, and our friend Yoina from Wierzbnik. I had not seen Moishe or Yoina during my time at Auschwitz-Birkenau or on the death march, but we were now reunited in Mauthausen. Although we were separated into different camps, I was comforted by the fact that they were still alive. It gave me hope that one day I would return to my town and find other family and friends there. We would see one another and know how the other had suffered at the hands of the Nazis, but we would perhaps resume our simple life in Wierzbnik, and things would somehow return to the way they were before. I was distracted by this delusion for just a moment until I remembered all the ashes I had seen rising from the smokestacks at Auschwitz-Birkenau, remembered all the bodies strewn along the side of the snowy roads during the death march, and until I remembered the trains that carried the Jews of Wierzbnik to Treblinka. At the very least, Moishe and Yoina were still alive, and that filled me with a small sliver of joy, even though I knew Moishe would never be reunited with his father, whom the Germans shot and killed the day of the liquidation of the Wierzbnik Ghetto while he was running to the labor camp.

Moishe and Yoina were sent to Camp II with the other able-bodied prisoners to work in the quarries or to fulfill other jobs.

A *kapo* from Birkenau had given Yoina something of value to smuggle into Mauthausen, but once inside, Yoina refused to relinquish it to the *kapo*, who wielded no power over his fellow inmates at Mauthausen. Yoina was able to trade on the black market for some extra rations, and even though our camps were divided by high stone walls, Yoina and my cousin Moishe would throw some bread over the wall for me when they could.

The barracks in Camp III were run by German criminals who wore triangle patches on their shirts. Jews wore yellow patches. Political prisoners wore red patches. Each group of prisoners could be identified by their patch. There were some 150 men in our barrack. The *blockalteste* was in charge of the barrack and the *kapo* ensured that prisoners followed the rules. There were no beds in the barracks, just a cold hard floor where we slept in rows, like herring. The *block-alteste* and *kapo*, two sadists, forced us to lie on our sides on the bare floor, with no room to move. Food was almost nonexistent in this camp. People fell dead around us all the time. We missed the watery soup and crumbling bread of Auschwitz-Birkenau.

Before the war, I would have been shocked and outraged at the site of dead bodies, but I had grown accustomed to the sights and smells. Was I losing touch with reality, with decency? How could I not find this despicable? How could I keep the images from penetrating my mind? I hoped for a day when this horror would end, and these scenes of dead bodies strewn around would stop and be erased from my thoughts. Those images constantly replayed for me in the daylight, and again in my sleep, but I could not escape them.

On Passover 1945, a mere skeleton of a man had stolen some potato peels and was eating them. He called to me by name, and asked me to lend him my spoon, which I did.

Who is this man? How does he know my name?

"I am Rachmir Wolfowitz," he said. I remembered him as an energetic member of the Jewish leadership of Wierzbnik. He was now a walking corpse, transformed into something grotesquely unrecognizable. I watched him greedily eat the cooked potato peels. Then, before I knew it, he leaned over and sucked in his last breath. He was gone. One minute, he was there with me, talking to me, the next, he was dead. Death could come for me soon too, but I continued to hope I could outrun it, at least a while longer.

Surely this horror cannot go on forever.

From a distance, I had seen people shot and killed. I had seen hangings. Wolfowitz's death was my first close-up encounter. I hoped he was now at peace and that his suffering had ceased.

Every morning at Mauthausen, the *kapos* chased us from our barracks and forced us to stand against the wall between Camp II and Camp III. The SS only came into the camp for roll calls. They had placed murderers in Mauthausen who willingly did their dirty work for them, and it was against this wall that many prisoners were shot. We huddled together, unsure whether we would be shot or permitted to live one more day. I had no purpose, no distraction, no work. All we did was stand against the wall with each other, freezing and hungry, taking turns blocking the cold wind from one another. One group would stand in front, then the others would exchange places. We had survived slave labor camps, and Auschwitz-Birkenau, but this camp reached yet another incomparable level of horror. This was a place of torture, brutality, and unspeakable abuse. I dreamed of a loaf of bread one night, but no longer dreamed of surviving the war, or of liberation.

Prisoners of Mauthausen were not expected to live. We were expected to die, whether by being worked to death, starved to death, or murdered. This was not a "work camp," in the sense of serving the Nazis in the war effort. This was a place designed to torment living souls until death was meted out. One effective method the Germans used to eliminate inmates was to douse them in water and leave them outside in the Austrian winter, as they had done to us upon our arrival, making us shower and then stand outside naked in the freezing air. Many prisoners died from hypothermia. We had no immunity. We were weak and malnourished.

Stay strong, move forward, don't look back, be smart, live, live, live.

I continued talking to myself to stay motivated and to keep moving forward.

As spring approached, a group of us were sent to the *Celten* Camp (Tent Camp). There were no barracks, just tents. The Tent Camp was filled with newly arrived prisoners from Hungary. These inmates were unaccustomed to camp life, and those of us who had already learned the ways of camp hierarchies and had experience with survival skills, took advantage of the new campers' inexperience. Not realizing the value of a real pair of leather shoes, the Hungarians would tie their shoes together with the laces and sling them over their shoulders. More seasoned prisoners easily stole the Hungarians' possessions, including their shoes, during the night when they, in a very civilized manner, left them unprotected. Hatred soon grew between the Hungarian and the Polish Jews.

Now we had gone from sleeping on the barrack floor to sleeping in tents. Food and water were scarce. We were not aiding the war effort, so our value to the Third Reich was waning. In the past we had prided ourselves on being somewhat indispensable, as we provided free labor for the German war effort, but now we were idle. We spent our time trying to avoid the barbaric *kapos*.

Spring brought renewed hope that perhaps soon the Allies would beat back the Germans, but I dared not dream of liberty or freedom. It was all I could do to persevere, to endure yet another roll call, to pass another day doing whatever possible to make myself invisible to the guards, and to merely exist.

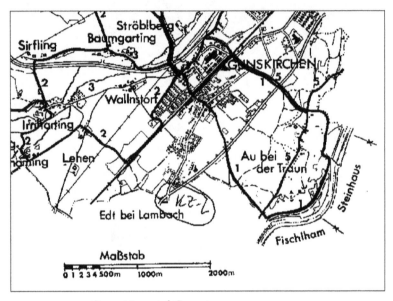

Gusen Memorial Committee - www.gusen.org.

"There is something in the human spirit that will survive and prevail. There is a tiny and brilliant light burning in the heart of man that will not go out no matter how dark the world becomes."

— Leo Tolstoy

GUNSKIRCHEN

IN MID-APRIL, WE were transferred to Gunskirchen, a fenced area in the forest, some thirty kilometers away from the main Mauthausen camp. This area was in a forest near Edt Bei Lambach, eleven miles from the town of Wels, and four miles north of Lambach. While preparing for the transport, I spied fighter planes overhead. The white smoke trailed behind as the plane progressed toward its destination.

Is this a German plane making a last ditch effort as the Allied forces advanced? Is this a Russian plane making headway into German-controlled area? Is this a British or American plane?

I sensed that the closing stage of the war was nearing, as we had long-awaited, and with that, our suffering might end. How much could a person withstand without breaking down or giving up? In Mauthausen, I wondered if the dead weren't the lucky ones.

During the march from Mauthausen to Gunskirchen, local Austrians threw bread from their rooftops, not so much because of their compassion or humanity, but because they took pleasure in seeing the inmates fight over a morsel or crumb. They jeered at the wretched group of prisoners passing by. I felt like an animal. I no longer felt like a human being. I was filthy, worn down, and painfully thin. I was mere skin and bones.

Gunskirchen, opened in March 1945, was designed as a construction camp to assist the German war industry. Construction was never finished, however, and it remained a primitive development without infrastructure, save for six or seven crudely made barracks with mud or stone floors, two auxiliary barracks, and one latrine with some twenty holes. The construction camp was not planned to hold 18,000 to 20,000 Jewish prisoners. There was no running water and no medical facility. Once a day, a truck delivered 1,500 liters of water for 18,000 hungry and thirsty prisoners to share. I had descended into something worse than hell on earth. Just as I could not fathom anything worse than Auschwitz-Birkenau when I first arrived at Mauthausen, now I could not believe that anything could be worse than the Tent Camp, but Gunskirchen proved me wrong yet again.

My fellow inmates were mostly Hungarians with professional degrees, all stripped of their dignity, all reduced to animals. Each barrack was originally built to house 300 people, but now many more than that were packed in, unable to breathe or move. I slept in the barracks one night and vowed to never again set foot inside. There were bodies three deep on the floor. Many were crushed to death during the night, and remained where they died. Despite the cold, I slept outside. The spring sun could not penetrate the thick canopy of the tall forest. Many others joined me, choosing to be exposed to the elements rather than suffer through the nightmare of the barracks with bodies strewn all around, some alive, some dead, and the stench of urine and feces and death that permeated the barracks. Even outside where I slept, I could not escape the stench of the creatures who bore no resemblance to the actual human beings they once were.

Even though I was relieved to be away from the *kapos* of Camp III, Gunskirchen was another step closer to death. In fact, I was descending into despair, thinking that death was preferable to this life.

There were roll calls at least three times a day, and food, if there was any, consisted of a piece of black bread and watery soup. Mockingly, we still carried with us at all times our *manashke* and spoon. They taunted us, wanting to be used, but we had nothing to use them for. My friend liked to say, "I invented escargot," as he dug his spoon into the ground. If he was fortunate enough to find any snails, he would devour them raw as though they were smothered in hot butter with garlic in a fine restaurant in Paris! We tried to find humor to lift our spirits, even in those darkest hours. Food and water were so sparse that prisoners were losing their minds. Some killed each other for a morsel of bread or a sip of water. All logic and reason were lost.

There were large pits where many were sent to work cutting stone. Many died performing work in the pits. We were fenced in with barbed wire and by an eight-foot-high wooden fence with watchtowers manned by SS guards armed with machine guns. There was no possibility of escape. There was only one way in and one way out, through a large wooden gate. The forest was dense. Barely any light came in. The ground was carpeted with pine needles.

I had endured much suffering until this point, but the physical pain eclipsed anything in my previous experience. My body hurt so badly that I couldn't differentiate the pain's origin. I just wanted the pain to stop.

Please stop the pain – once and for all.

The death toll rose. Two to three hundred prisoners died each day from dysentery or typhoid. In a period of three weeks, approximately five thousand people died of starvation and sickness. Without food and water, we ate leaves off the trees and drank rainwater when it fell from the sky. Everyone suffered terribly from diarrhea. Many died during the nights. We were constantly stepping over dead bodies. If we awakened next to a corpse, one of us would grab the stiff body by the arms, the other by the legs, and we would unceremoniously discard it in a large pit. These bodies weighed almost nothing, being little more than bones. Any sense of civility was lost; we were numb, immune to the horror of callously tossing aside a human being like garbage into a landfill. I could not dwell on the situation. I had to make it through another moment, another hour, another day. For all I knew, I could be tomorrow's dead.

Managing the pangs of hunger in my belly was challenge enough, but one thing incomparable, and unbearable, was thirst. In the last days before liberation, there was neither food nor water. I became extremely dehydrated and suffered from headaches, fatigue, dizziness, and hallucinations. There is no way to describe the anguish of a dry mouth, a dry tongue, and the cracked and parched lips that occur when your body stops producing saliva. The lack of water was driving me close to the edge of sanity as my body began shutting down from the extreme deprivation. Years of malnourishment, disease, exposure to harsh temperatures and lack of proper clothing, not to mention exhaustion from the death march, and years of hard labor, caused many to faint and to lapse into unconsciousness or convulsions. The lack of water more than anything was taking its toll on me physically and mentally.

The smell of Gunskirchen was nauseating. We were wearing the same tattered, unwashed clothes we had worn for months. We would take off our uniform shirts and shake them out, hoping to rid ourselves of some of the lice that were viciously biting, eating us up alive. The stench of Gunskirchen was a combination of body odor, mud, urine, feces, and rotting corpses, along with the cloying smell of German tobacco that the guards smoked.

Truth is often more unbelievable than fiction, and there are things we experienced at Gunskirchen that defy a rational person's belief system. Our minds did not want to register the atrocities we witnessed. In all the years of the war, I had always thought about living, about surviving. I had never longed for death – not until the last three weeks of the war, when I was struck by dysentery, unable to move, lying in filth, covered with lice, hungry, thirsty, tired. I lay there involuntarily breathing in, breathing out, unsure of when my last breath would be, but feeling that death was near. Very near. I existed moment to moment.

I wish it would all end. Please just let the agony end. Let it be over. I have no more strength, no more will. I cannot take any more suffering.

I am no longer human. I am drifting to another dimension. All that is left of me is my spirit, which is readying to leave my physical body. I have nothing left to live for. Even if I survive, will anyone else from my family remain? I have no home. Poland is finished for the Jews. Where will I go? What will become of me? Better to close my eyes and let my soul drift into the next world…

As the war was coming to an end, and the Germans wanted to hide the evidence of their crimes, they forced the stronger inmates to dig deep pits to bury the dead in mass graves. There were bodies everywhere. Just outside the camp, in the woods, bodies piled up. Prisoners were forced to dig mass graves behind the barracks, but these were not sufficient in capacity. The graves filled up quickly. The SS-guards treated us harshly, even down to the very last day. The camp commander, an SS-lieutenant whose name I never knew, but I suspect I would recognize his face even today, treated us as his personal property. I heard a rumor after liberation that the camp commander sent emissaries to the approaching Allied troops, purporting to have orders from his superiors to torch the camp with all of us locked in, rather than surrender, and offering our lives in exchange for his and his men's freedom from capture. I have no way of knowing whether there was any truth to these rumors.

This much I knew: time was running out for me. I had reached a point of indescribable despondency and anguish.

United States Holocaust Memorial Museum
Collection, Gift of Horace S. Berry

"The last of the human freedoms – to choose one's attitude
in any given set of circumstances, to choose one's own way."

— Dr. Viktor Frankl

LIBERATION

AT THE BEGINNING of May 1945, we sensed that something major was occurring when the German guards abandoned their posts in the watchtower, and many of the SS troops evacuated their posts and left the camp.

On May 4th, the 71st United States Army Infantry arrived at Gunskirchen, after low-flying Allied planes dropped bombs around the camp. Sadly, some prisoners were killed during the bombing. At the entrance of the camp, I witnessed distraught prisoners devouring the carcass of a horse that had been killed in the bombing. Prisoners were out of their minds from starvation and abuse. And when I thought I could not see anything worse in this lifetime, I witnessed crazed prisoners eating the flesh of dead humans whose bodies had been split apart and splattered across the barbed wire fence from the bomb blasts.

Do my eyes deceive me? Can these people be so deprived and so depraved that they are eating human flesh?

I wish it were not true, and I wish I could un-see those images, but I am a witness to the fact that it happened. Regrettably, my eyes saw those sights, although my head and heart wish to believe otherwise. People were desperate beyond the normal bounds of human reason.

Allied soldiers entered the camp and announced that we were

free. When they arrived, they found us in this deplorable condition. The deprivation, abuse, overcrowding, and dead bodies strewn about had caused some prisoners to descend into madness. The Allied soldiers gave prisoners candy and whatever food or water they had with them. They gave us cigarettes, which some prisoners ingested rather than smoked – anything to satiate the pain of hunger. A brigade of African-American soldiers gave us food, chewing gum, chocolates, shoes, and, literally, the clothes off their backs. The liberators arrived in Jeeps and told us to remain where we were, that they would bring medical assistance, food, and water. Many newly freed prisoners wandered from the camp, crawling, walking, dragging themselves from bondage, but many enjoyed only minutes of freedom before dying just outside the camp entrance, or along the road to the nearby town. At least they perished with the knowledge that they died as free men.

Freedom, sweet Freedom, finally, no more suffering. Relief. Breathe.

I felt a sense of relief, but I was not entirely comforted: I was far from home. Home? What does that mean, home? There was no going home. I had witnessed the Jewish community of Wierzbnik being forced onto that train. There was no going home. There was no home. Poland represented the death of everything and nearly everyone I had ever known.

May 4, 1945 is my "re-birth day." I was fourteen years old and weighed less than 100 pounds. Maybe less than 90. I was a layer of skin stretched over a skeleton. The munitions boxes I had built at Tartak were my pyramids, the open gates at Gunskirchen my Red Sea. I was once a slave in the land of the Third Reich. Now I was free, but free to go where? To do what? I knew that my brother, my two grandmothers, my grandfather, father, uncle, and most of my family and friends were dead. I did not believe that my mother, thirty-seven years old, could have survived Auschwitz, let alone the death march, so I presumed that she, too, had perished.

After surviving Auschwitz-Birkenau and the death march, my uncle Ben Zion was sent to Ebensee, an underground camp where he and other prisoners were forced to make airplane parts. Tragically, my uncle, who had saved my life when he bribed the *kapo* with the gold coin, and had sacrificed and suffered so much, died just one day before the liberation of Mauthausen.

On that first night of freedom, I was too weak to go anywhere. Many of the prisoners were too ill to move, so remarkably we spent the night in the camp. We were a pitiful sight with a wretched smell, crawling with lice, barely passable as human beings. The transition from an animalistic survival mode of existence to that of rational, optimistic human beings would be slow and painful. We were no longer prisoners of the Nazi war machine, but we were devastated physically, mentally, spiritually. We remained psychological prisoners of all that we had witnessed, experienced, all that we had become. Anti-Semitism still existed in Germany, Poland, and among Nazi sympathizers, allowing many of the perpetrators to slip back into society as if they had played no role in the atrocities.

The next morning, on my first day of freedom, the Americans took us to Hirsching, Austria, where there was a military airport with barracks. The Americans had been using the airport to fly in food and supplies for the Army and were now using it as part of the humanitarian relief effort. One of the first things we did was to burn our clothes. This action was mostly to disinfect ourselves of lice and filth, but also helped us mark a transition from slavery to freedom.

For the next few weeks there, I began to recover from the physical and mental torment of the prior six years, from the time the Germans invaded Poland when I was but nine years old, to the time of my liberation from Gunskirchen, when I was just shy of my fifteenth birthday. My youth allowed my body to heal quickly, to recover from the trauma of the previous years. I gained weight and felt stronger with each passing day. It was more difficult, however, for the older men to return to their former physical state, even those just a few years older.

During those first few weeks after liberation, we struggled to get our bearings. We relished our freedom, but grappled with the new reality that had become our lives. I had some friends with me at the time of liberation from Gunskirchen, including my former neighbors from Wierzbnik, Herschl Tannenbaum and his brother, Mendel. They were fortunate to have remained together throughout the war, lucky to have even one surviving family member. They always looked out for me, even when we were in Birkenau together. Mendel told me that he had even helped seek out *Kapo* Yignatz, to save me from the gas chambers on *Yom Kippur*. We had been liberated, but we remained in survival mode, fending for ourselves. Herschl, a few years my senior, stole rations from the military barracks that he shared with the rest of us. Every bit of nourishment helped to strengthen us, but many who survived the war succumbed because they were unable to digest the food provided during liberation. Zvi, for example, became deathly ill from eating a tub of margarine. A U.S. Army doctor saved his life. I also learned after liberation that Max Naiman, also of Wierzbnik, was with us in Gunskirchen, although I do not recall seeing him. We had become unrecognizable shells of our former selves, forlorn eyes in skulls atop living skeletons.

The Americans relocated us to Wells, Austria. There were so many wounded who needed care, but at the same time, the U.S. Army vigorously pursued Nazi perpetrators before too many of them could escape justice or slip undetected into *normal* society. In Wells, we met soldiers from a Jewish brigade that had fought alongside the British. Their mission was to discourage survivors from returning to their hometowns or from remaining in Europe. They wanted survivors to join them in Palestine and aid them in their quest for a Jewish homeland.

Herschl Tannenbaum was eager to leave this part of Europe, and said, "Let's go to Italy." That could be the first leg of our Journey to Palestine. I had nothing to lose; in fact, I had nothing at all. No family, no home. I had no wish to stay in Europe or Poland, and as a child I remember hearing older Jews talking about the dream of Zionism. My parents had never spoken of Zionism or of Palestine as somewhere they aspired to move. They were entrenched in Poland and assumed they would live a long life in our idyllic town. They did have family who had emigrated to the United States, and it was conceivable for me to seek them out and try to make my way there, but I decided I would stay with my comrades from the camps, and start anew in the Promised Land.

The British permitted only 1,500 Jews per month into Palestine, so it would be difficult to obtain documentation. We would take our chances, our small band of disheveled and broken young men.

The Brigade loaded trucks with those of us willing to attempt the journey. They drove the few hundred of us who were willing to take the risk to Augsburg, Austria. There, we were hidden in three train cars interspersed between cars carrying goods. Our voyage was clandestine, but now *we* closed the doors to the train cars from the *inside*, and we were traveling in a freight train, not cattle cars. There was probably some risk in crossing the borders without papers, but it was a time of such chaos and corruption that the Brigade could utilize its resources to ensure our passage. The train traveled throughout the night, carrying us away from Austria, Germany, Poland – away from the Jewish cemetery that Europe had become.

At the time of the liquidation of the Wierzbnik Ghetto, there were some 4,500 to 5,000 Jews living there. Of those who survived the selection and liquidation of Wierzbnik and who were sent to the Starachowice camps, only half survived Auschwitz-Birkenau. Of the lucky few who survived Auschwitz-Birkenau, only about 500 of us remained after the war. After liberation, many died from the years of maltreatment, and others were killed by Poles, even after the German retreat. Freedom had come at last, but at a steep price. European Jewry had been nearly annihilated. I had beaten the unlikely odds of surviving, and now I was beginning a journey that would eventually take me to the Promised Land, where the future awaited.

From the private collection of Martin Baranek.

*"Nobody is stronger, nobody is weaker than someone who
came back. There is nothing you can do to such a person
because whatever you could do is less than what has already
been done to him. We have already paid the price."*

— Elie Wiesel

ITALY

AFTER THE OVERNIGHT train ride, we arrived in Bologna, Italy. From there we transported by truck to Modena, where the Brigade had taken over an old Italian *Academia Militare*. The Brigade took charge of the building and used it to house refugees. We slept on the floor with blankets. It was there in Modena that Herschl bought me my first new pair of shoes since the liquidation of Wierzbnik on October 27, 1942. I took pleasure in the luxury of my new shoes. My mind turned to Shimmale, the shoemaker from Wierzbnik who used to make shoes for my family, and I wondered about his fate.

After the war, people desperately searched for information about loved ones. I met someone in Modena who had been with my father at Buna. He confirmed what I had feared, that my father had become another victim. I was alone in the world, adrift in a sea of other lost souls. Zvi Unger heard that there was more opportunity for us in Rome, so we decided to take our chances there. I already spoke Yiddish, Polish, and German, and was learning enough Italian to get by. We had no money for train tickets, but we also had no fear, so when the train conductor asked for our tickets, *"billete, billete,"* we simply handed him a page from a *Siddur*, a Jewish prayer book written in Hebrew that the American soldiers had given us, confidently proffering it as if it were some sort of U.S. or Allied pass.

In Rome, we met other refugees who allowed us to stay with

them on the floor of their *pensione*. Many organizations were already assisting survivors and refugees. The United Nations Relief Agency (U.N.R.A.), and the Joint Distribution Committee, commonly referred to as *"The Joint,"* provided us with T-shirts, underwear, and other basic supplies. We began selling these wares to local Italians. Zvi Unger and I had saved up enough money to get our own hotel room. We kept going back to U.N.R.A. for handouts, giving a different name each time to receive a parcel. We were gathering an inventory that we kept in our hotel room.

We traveled all over Rome on the streetcars. When asked for our *"billete,"* we simply responded *"Prisionero Tedesco,"* German prisoner, and the Italian train conductors left us alone. We had no money to buy food, so we often took advantage of our Italian hosts by eating in their cafes and restaurants, sneaking out before the check arrived. At this stage of my life, I looked for shortcuts, but only to satisfy my hunger. I had no interest in cheating anyone. I was still in survival mode, utilizing the skills I had learned during my years navigating the camps.

The Vatican began baptizing refugees, especially children, paying them 30,000 lire for undergoing the process, so we decided to "convert." We stood before a priest who uttered a few incantations in Latin, waved his hands in front of us, splashed some holy water on us, and declared us Catholics. We collected our 30,000 lire each and went on our way, knowing full well that once a Jew, always a Jew, no matter what the Vatican decreed. Hitler cared not if someone had converted. All that mattered was whether someone had Jewish blood running through their veins, no matter how diluted.

We had become so good at using false names with the U.N.R.A. and successfully going back many times undetected, we thought we would try to be converted by the Vatican a second time. However, I was easy to recognize due to my small stature, so when I went back to try and collect another 30,000 lire, someone from the church recognized me, and I was forced to run from there. The last thing I wanted to do was to survive the Nazis just to end up in an Italian jail.

Later, I was overcome with an unknown illness. All I remember is a high fever. Zvi took me to a local hospital, which transferred me to another hospital run by nuns. I communicated with the nuns in German, but could not understand their Italian, nor discern what was ailing me. After two weeks in the hospital, feeling better and having regained my strength, the doctors discharged me. Zvi arrived at the hospital to pick me up.

"We are out of business," he announced. "Someone stole our inventory from our hotel room." As disappointing as the news was, I felt hopeful that we at least had something to look forward to in terms of reaching Palestine.

On *Yom Kippur* 1945, having recently turned fifteen, I, along with my band of refugee brothers, entered the Grand Synagogue of Rome. I stayed for about fifteen minutes. I felt compelled to go to *shul,* more for the sake of tradition and out of respect to my departed parents and grandparents, but not out of any religious fervor, and certainly not for God. I was not about to ask God to forgive my sins, not when that same God allowed the brutal murder of one and a half million Jewish children, like my brother, Chaskel. I did feel grateful though to think back on the year that had passed since the previous *Yom Kippur* holiday, when I was saved from the quarantine barrack. How close to death I had been, and now, here I stood – a free man, able to go to a *shul.* Did any synagogues even remain standing in Poland or Germany? It was a remarkable gift to freely attend a Jewish service, given how practicing Judaism, even possessing any Jewish objects, (a prayer book, *tefillin,* etc.) could have resulted in death in the ghetto and in the camps.

I sensed that my luck in Rome was running out – I had almost been caught at the Vatican for trying to collect the conversion money twice, I had skipped out on numerous tabs at local restaurants, our inventory of goods from U.N.R.A. had been stolen, and I had just spent two weeks in an Italian hospital speaking German, a language that I could no longer bear to hear, let alone speak. The time had come for me to get on a better path.

"Zvi," I said, "I heard about a school in the South in Santa Maria al Bagno. I think we should make our way down there. Other young survivors are going there, and the Brigade is helping them get to Palestine."

But Zvi refused to go with me. "Michulek, I must return to Germany to look for my dear sister. I have heard rumors that she may have survived. I too wish to make my way to Palestine, but first, before I leave the graveyard of Europe behind me, I must know for sure if I have any surviving family members, and if it is true that my sister has survived, I must find her. You have been like a brother to me, and if you go to Palestine, I will find you there. Now, I want to give you this small sum of money to go by way of Bari to Santa Maria al Bagno."

Again, another goodbye. It was hard to bid farewell to my comrades from the camps, but especially those like Kiva, Herschl, Mendel, and Zvi whom I knew from childhood in Wierzbnik. They knew me when I was a part of a family, part of a community. Now here I was alone in the world, charting a new path for myself.

Santa Maria al Bagno was a respite from the outside world. There, hundreds of young survivors, between fifteen and seventeen years old, recuperated and began planning their futures. There were eight groups, each with a Hebrew name: *Hatikvah* ("The Hope"), *Geulim* ("Redeemed"), *Gur Ariyeh* ("Young Lions"), *Atid* ("Future"), *Moledet* ("Homeland"), *Tzabarim* ("Native of Land of Israel"), *Dror* ("Liberty"), *and Frumka,* which was for girls, although I do not recall ever seeing girls during my stay at Santa Maria. I was in the aptly named *Geulim.*

Other than my hospital stay, it was in Santa Maria where I slept, for the first time since my liberation, in an actual bed with linen sheets. It was a small but important comfort. I was beginning to feel human again, and to take delight in the luxury of something

I had once taken for granted. There were thirty-five of us in *Geulim*. We stayed together at Santa Maria and throughout our Journey to Palestine, where we were split into two groups that went to separate Kibbutzim.

Throughout the war, I had heard many rumors. Rumors about where various transports were going, where the train cars were headed, which towns no longer existed, which towns in Eastern Germany now held prisoners, etc. It was only at Santa Maria that I first learned of Treblinka.

Treblinka was comprised of a forced labor camp and a death camp. German and Ukrainian guards operated the camp. Barbed wire surrounded the camp, with tree branches interspersed throughout the wire in order to camouflage the fence and to obstruct any view of the camp from the outside. The camp was in a fairly remote area, about twelve miles northwest of the village of Treblinka. There was a train platform and barracks for sorting prisoners' belongings and a simulated train station, to deceive prisoners into believing they were in fact being transported to other locales. Upon exiting the trains, men were separated from women and children, under the lashes of Nazi whips and the barked orders of Nazi and Ukrainian guards. The platform held discarded clothing and other items. Guards told the prisoners that they needed to shower for hygiene purposes, before being transferred to various labor camps. Guards instructed the prisoners to undress rapidly. Prisoners made their way through "The Tube" that led directly to the gas chambers. Guards forcefully escorted those who were too old or too infirm to make their way through "The Tube" to a "reception area" instead where they were shot in the back of the neck before their bodies were tossed into a fire pit.

Treblinka existed as a place to conduct mass murder. German efficiency perfected the killings of 2,000 to 3,000 Jews in an hour and a half. The Germans eventually increased the capacity of the gas chambers to accommodate 3,800 people at once. More than 900,000 Jews were killed in assembly-line fashion there in less than one year.

Some desperate prisoners staged a revolt on August 2, 1943, without much success. Few of the prisoners involved in the uprising survived, but the Germans knew they needed to eliminate as much of the evidence of Treblinka's horrors as possible. They exhumed the bodies from mass graves and cremated them; they dismantled and destroyed the camp's structures, and they ploughed the land and planted trees in an attempt to conceal their inhumane crimes.

Treblinka became the final resting place of both of my grandmothers, my grandfather, aunts, uncles, cousins, friends, classmates, and my younger brother, the baby of the family, Chaskel. And so, the day of the liquidation of the Wierzbnik Ghetto, October 27th, the 16th day of *Cheshvan* on the Jewish calendar, is the day that the Jews of Wierzbnik commemorate the yahrzeits, the anniversary of the deaths of our family members. This is the date when we say *Kaddish*, the mourner's prayer for the dead, for the death of the Jewish community of Wierzbnik.

After learning about Treblinka for the first time, and finally knowing the fate of my beloved family, my beloved Wierzbnik, I began to say *Kaddish* for those whom I had lost.

At Santa Maria, we studied Hebrew, ate together in a common dining room, and raised the flag that would one day be the official flag of the State of Israel. We established routines and began the arduous process of healing from years of trauma. Physically, I was gaining weight and returning, more or less, to *normal*. But what does that mean? What is *normal*? Nobody survived the Holocaust and remained *normal*.

Many kids at Santa Maria had nightmares. Nearly all had difficulty sleeping. Once asleep, many cried out in the night for their parents or siblings, or they screamed out in terror as they remembered their ordeals. I, too, suffered from nightmares, especially after learning about Treblinka, and found myself replaying certain images in my mind over and over again.

After nine months at Santa Maria, our visas to Palestine had still not come through. The British were severely limiting the number of refugees or displaced persons who could legally enter British-controlled Palestine. Other countries, the United States included, also limited the numbers of legal immigrants. We were in a state of limbo: no family, no home, no country.

Seven of the eight groups from Santa Maria received legal papers to emigrate to Palestine – only *Geulim*, my group, did not get official documents, and so we were the only group to go to Palestine clandestinely. Our journey would be grueling. There was the risk that we would be intercepted by the British, returned to Europe, interned at a DP camp, or incarcerated. We wanted to get on with our lives, but encountered difficulties and stumbling blocks at each turn.

Would there ever be justice for us, the people who had had suffered so much?

I continued to talk to myself, willing myself to keep moving forward, step by step, toward my uncertain future.

"Just as man cannot live without dreams, he cannot live without hope. If dreams reflect the past, hope summons the future."

— Elie Wiesel

JOURNEY TO PALESTINE

THE BRITISH WERE watching our every move, so after two or three nights of false starts, the *Kaf Gimel* departed from the port of Bocca di Magra. We left in the dead of night, when we were less likely to be detected. We boarded small rowboats that shuttled us to the awaiting *Kaf Gimel Yordei Ha'Sira,* "The 23 Seamen." The *Kaf Gimel,* which held 790 refugees of all ages, was one of nearly one hundred or so boats that transported Jewish refugees from Europe to the unpredictable frontier of Palestine.

The vessel was named in memory of twenty-three members of the *Haganah* who lost their lives, along with a British major, on a ship that departed Haifa on May 18, 1941, and went down during a mission against the Vichy French Forces.

The war left us shattered, but we had begun the long, arduous process of creating new lives for ourselves. After years of torture and trauma, we embarked on yet another journey of survival. *Bricha,* meaning flight or escape, was the name of the organized, yet clandestine, emigration of survivors from Europe to Allied-occupied areas and to Palestine. Although Britain was part of the Allied Forces and controlled Palestine, they too limited the number of Jewish refugees who could legally immigrate. Those who went with legal documentation were known as *Aliyah Aleph,* but many resorted to entering illegally, as was the case with *Geulim,* in an effort known as *Aliyah*

Bet. The British intercepted many boats carrying illegal refugees, who were often repatriated to Europe and incarcerated, or held in detention camps in Cyprus or elsewhere.

Few of us had ever ventured on the rough Mediterranean waters, and most of us were overcome by seasickness. The toilets were below deck, where quarters were cramped and the air was stale. Soon, the toilets were all clogged, so some of the adults took wooden two-by-fours and constructed rudimentary "toilets," hanging them over the side of the ship, and draping them with blankets to provide for some privacy. Little by little, we were restoring our sense of dignity and self-consciousness following years of extreme humiliation.

Refusing to go below deck, I gathered what few things I had with me, staked out a corner on the upper deck, and remained there for twelve long rocking days and nights. The motion of the sea did little to soothe me; on the contrary, for most of the journey, it contributed to my distress.

As we neared Turkey, the ship broke down and we drifted for three days. We sent out an SOS and waited for the *Haganah* and other volunteers to bring us tools and functioning motors. As we waited in the hot summer sun, rocking back and forth, we spied low-flying British airplanes. With no place to hide, the British caught us. Although it may seem unimaginable, after fighting with the Allies to defeat Hitler, the British rammed or bombed boats carrying refugees, causing many to drown. Who would have thought that survivors of the Nazis could perish at the hands of our so-called *allies?*

The British towed the *Kaf Gimel* to the Port of Haifa, where we anchored. We could see the Land of Milk and Honey; it was within our grasp, but we were not permitted to disembark. Like Moses, we stood on the threshold of the Promised Land, but were unable to enter. At least we could taste the sweetness of tomatoes grown in the Holy Land that volunteers brought to the ship, along with cases of food and other supplies. We had food and water on board the ship, but it was not sufficient for the length of the journey, which was not expected to last two weeks. Volunteers brought provisions at just the right moment, as supplies were running low, and water had to be rationed.

The motors never arrived. The British forced us off the *Kaf Gimel* and onto their warship, which carried us to Cyprus. Before August 1946, illegal refugees who made it to Palestine were taken to a processing center called Atlit before being released by the British. After that time, the British stopped accepting illegal refugees at Atlit, but sent them to Cyprus instead. The *Kaf Gimel* was one of the first ships sent to Cyprus. We arrived there on my sixteenth birthday, August 15, 1946. At that time, the British permitted 1,500 Jews per month into Palestine – 750 from Cyprus and 750 from displaced persons (DP) camps in Europe. We were interred at *Famagusta*, a camp surrounded by barbed wire and soldiers in watchtowers.

This cannot possibly be happening. I cannot possibly be back in a camp surrounded by barbed wire, without freedom once again. Have I come all this way to have only gone backward? When will this nightmare end?

We were still prisoners; still not free, but thankfully we were no longer rocking on the interminable waves of the Mediterranean Sea. From within *Famagusta*, we organized demonstrations at the fence surrounding the camp. The facilities were minimal, and we had no showers, so the guards led us to the sea to bathe. We had passes that allowed us to enter and exit the camp for these outings. On our weekly swimming expeditions, we would hide our passes in a box of matches. Upon exiting the camp, we would throw the box of matches over the fence in order for others to use our exit passes. This was especially important for the crew of the ship. The crew was made up mostly of Italians, Greeks, and some Jewish leadership from the *Haganah*. We needed to get the crew out, so that they could continue their heroic work of returning to Europe to transport more of our survivor brethren.

During the three months that we remained on Cyprus, we continued to learn Hebrew and prepare for what lay ahead for us in Palestine. Little did we anticipate that we would soon need to take up arms and fight a new war – Israel's War of Independence.

Finally, in November, we received the long-anticipated wonderful news that our papers were in order and that we were going to Palestine – legally.

From the private collection of Martin Baranek.

"If you will it, it is no dream; and if you do not will it, a dream it is and a dream it will stay."Theodor Herzl, "Altneuland," 1902.

PALESTINE

WHEN WE ARRIVED in Palestine, it was not the Zion that we had read about in the poetry of Maimonides. It was not the Land of Milk and Honey as our forefathers in the *shtetls* and *shtiebels* of Poland and Eastern Europe had described.

We were not exactly met with open arms or open hearts when we arrived on a British warship at the port of Haifa. British soldiers took us in trucks to *Atlit,* a former military camp on a twenty-five-acre parcel of land adjacent to the Mediterranean. The British Mandate built *Atlit* in the late 1930s. It was converted into a detention camp for both legal and illegal immigrants with entry certificates.

Once again, we found ourselves behind barbed wire, with guards in watchtowers. Although we were in the land of *Eretz Yisrael,* it was almost too much to endure psychologically after all we had been through.

Only those with family who would claim or sponsor an immigrant were immediately released. Those without family were left in *Atlit* to be processed at some later date. My cousin, Arieh Kopf, found out that I was being held in *Atlit,* so he and his fiancée came to visit every Saturday, sometimes with gifts of chocolate.

After 30 days of quarantine at *Atlit,* the camp administration finally released my band of brothers from Santa Maria. The British issued us identification cards. A group from Kibbutz Sarid, a Shomer

Hatzair *kibbutz*, founded by Latvian Jews in the 1920s and later joined by wealthy German Jews who immigrated to Palestine before Hitler's rise to power, met us at *Atlit* to claim us. They transported us by trucks to the *kibbutz*, located between Haifa and Afula. Thirty-five of us from Santa Maria remained together at Sarid; another group from Santa Maria went to a *kibbutz* near Afula called Misra.

The founders of the *kibbutz* Sarid prepared a party for our arrival. We were the first group of war refugees to arrive at Sarid. There were approximately 300 members of *kibbutz* Sarid. Although it was an agricultural *kibbutz*, its members were educated. Every Friday night, they brought in guest speakers to the dining hall and sometimes orchestras performed. There was a social hall where we played ping-pong, and with money we earned by digging out potatoes, we bought a record player. We volunteered to work on Saturdays to relieve other workers from the *kibbutz*, so they could build a swimming pool.

How far we had come; how modern our new lives.

Of my roommates, my friend, Arie Wachsman, whom I knew from Birkenau, remained on the *kibbutz*. He later founded his own *kibbutz*. Another friend, Alex, who played the accordion, became a policeman. Everyone was figuring out who they were and who they wanted to be. We were in the process of becoming our adult selves. It was an extremely challenging time without the love or guidance of family.

At the *kibbutz* there was a housemother who was supposed to look after us. She was exceptionally kind, but what could she and the other leaders of the *kibbutz* know about caring for orphaned concentration camp survivors who had seen pure evil? There was no psychological counseling, and even if there had been, many of us didn't think we needed it. After what we had survived, we certainly weren't going to take advice from anyone who had not seen the inside of a concentration camp. We all would have benefited from counseling, but many of us were too traumatized to reveal to another human being the profound depths of our suffering. We could not verbalize what we had experienced. Could anyone who had not been with us even believe us? We were hardened, broken, damaged. I was unsure whether we could be made whole.

Students from other *kibbutzim* came to Sarid to study together in a high school. Refugees had a separate school. We studied four hours a day and worked four hours a day in the fields, feeding cows and sheep and riding horses. At the time, the *kibbutz* was strictly agricultural, growing grapes, apples, and vegetables. The *kibbutz* also had dairy cows for milk production.

At the *kibbutz*, there was no focus on religion, but schoolteachers were brought in who shared the teachings of Marx, Lenin, and Engel. We also studied history, math, literature, and Hebrew. Left-wing organizers were scouting the *kibbutz*, and they gave me the opportunity to go to school for three years at *Mossad Chinuchi*. I chose instead to go for two years to *Aliyat Noar* with the boys who were with me on the journey from Italy. This was a youth program to learn Hebrew, mathematics, and science. I was not yet eighteen, but my studies had been interrupted by the war, and even though *Aliyat Noar* did not confer diplomas, it provided us much-needed structure and regularity.

There was a big sign in the social hall that read *"Hebrew Only – No Yiddish."* The foundation from the *cheder* in Wierzbnik had held me in good stead, and thankfully, I picked up Hebrew with ease. Yiddish was the language of Eastern European Jews, but with the majority of Europe's Jews in mass graves or in ashes, the language was sure to die as well, especially as the Jews of Palestine favored the Biblical language of Hebrew.

We were still in the arduous process of shifting from camp mentality to a mentality of freedom. We caused problems for the leaders of the *kibbutz* as we lacked conscience and self-discipline. We tried their patience.

Each Friday we received fresh laundry. At first, we were afraid to give up the T-shirts that The Joint gave us because we feared we might not get them back. Having previously lost all our possessions, we became possessive of those few material items we could call our own.

On days off, we were free to do as we pleased. It cost about one pound or one pound fifty sterling, the British currency, for a bus ticket to Tel Aviv. Given the likely possibility of an impending war for independence, a curfew of 4:00 p.m. was announced for Tel Aviv. One day, I was stuck in Tel Aviv after curfew, and could not return to the *kibbutz*. I had the phone number of a woman from Wierzbnik who was working as a maid in a doctor's home. She paid for a room on Shanken Street, where I stayed for the night. In addition, she gave me five pounds sterling, probably half a month's salary for her. Back in Wierzbnik, my father, who had inherited his mother's generous nature, often anonymously helped friends and relatives in need. In this way, the recipients of his charity and kindness could maintain their dignity and not feel embarrassed by their need for assistance. I later learned that my father had, in fact, helped this woman who was now able to return the favor.

The British were readying themselves to depart from Palestine. The Arabs had begun attacking Jewish settlements and *kibbutzim*, and a group of us were faced with the decision to remain at Sarid to defend the *kibbutz,* or to go to the border and volunteer to fight the Arabs. Soon enough, conscription into the nascent army would be mandatory. The majority of us didn't have anyone; we were self-sufficient, defensive, selfish, and possessed by a survivor mentality. We may not have had any blood relatives, but we had each other for family. We had bonded through our time at Santa Maria, Cyprus, *Atlit*, and now the *kibbutz,* and we were determined to remain together.

We were adjusting to so many new things in our lives including the *kibbutz,* a new language, a new rhythm of life. We knew about the conflict between the Arabs and the Jews that began in 1917 with the Balfour Declaration and the 1920 creation of the British Mandate of Palestine, but we were solely focused on our own survival during

World War II and heard nothing of what was happening in Palestine during that time. It was only afterward, when the Brigade convinced us to resettle in Palestine, that we paid proper attention to what was happening there. We learned that there was not only tension between the Arabs and the Jews, but also between each of them and the British forces. Both the Arabs and the Jews were dissatisfied with British policies, and the Arabs revolted and Jewish resistance began.

After the United Nations adopted the Partition Plan for Palestine on November 29, 1947, civil war broke out. The U.N. Plan called for the division of Palestine into three areas: an Arab state, a Jewish state, and the Special International Regime for the cities of Jerusalem and Bethlehem. The Arabs, of course, rejected the U.N. Partition Plan, and the Arab Higher Committee's spokesperson, Jamal Husseini said the Arabs would drench "the soil of our beloved country with the last drop of our blood." Clerics in Egypt called for *jihad,* holy war, against the Jews. We were once again thrust into chaos and war.

On Friday evening, May 14, 1948, the date the British officially vacated Palestine, David Ben-Gurion announced Israel's independence. The United States, the Soviet Union, and many other countries immediately recognized the State of Israel. I was at Sarid, on patrol duty in the fields, when I heard the remarkable news. But not everyone appreciated the fact that the Jews finally had a homeland. Violence immediately erupted between the Arabs and the Jews. The British did not intervene except to protect their own forces and their own interests. Ben Gurion's declaration ignited all-out war for an independent State of Israel. Egypt, Transjordan, Syria, and Iraq sent their armies to invade.

The Secretary-General of the Arab League, Azzam Pasha, declared, not unlike Hitler in his manifesto *Mein Kampf,* "It will be a war of annihilation. It will be a momentous massacre in history that will be talked about like the massacres of the Mongols or the Crusades."

From one country to another, one continent to another, one religion to another – more pronouncements of hatred towards the Jews. What have we done to provoke such hostility from our Christian and Muslim brothers? Regardless of the motives, one lesson from the Holocaust learned: when a madman openly states his anti-Semitic intentions, listen to him, believe him, and do not take his rantings as those of a harmless fanatic. Take it as a warning. Get prepared to get out, or to stand your ground and fight!

Thirty-five of us at Sarid took a vote on what to do. We told the *madrich,* our teacher, that we wanted to volunteer for *Palmach,* a precursor to the Israel Defense Forces. All thirty-five of us from Santa Maria joined the 8th *Gdud,* or battalion, of *Hativat Ha'Negev.* We were able to remain together as a unit in the *Palmach,* the fighting force of the *Haganah.*

Two days after Ben Gurion's declaration, *Palmach* leaders sent us to Be'er Yakov, near Rechovot, for two weeks of combat training. They taught us how to read maps and find our way according to the position of the sun. They taught us how to use weapons and take apart and reassemble rifles. They taught us Morse Code and how to use walkie-talkies. It was an honor for us to serve in the Army, however rudimentary, serving alongside brave men and women to ensure a Jewish homeland. If there had been a place for Jews to have called home in the 1930s, perhaps many more souls would have been saved. Before the establishment of the State of Israel, however, many countries denied Jews citizenship or entry. Only a Jewish state could ensure citizenship for the Jews of the world. I was determined to fight for a cause I deeply believed in.

The military was still in the early stages of development. Before leaving for the Negev in the south, we received arms shipments from Czechoslovakia, but we still lacked uniforms and other basic equipment and supplies. The Negev was a vast remote territory without much of a Jewish population, and when we arrived, we were surrounded by Arab fighters.

In the middle of the night, we crossed the Egyptian lines, a successful strategy, because the Egyptians did not fight at night. We fought fiercely for three to four weeks in al-Fallujah. The Egyptians had laid mines around the area causing many casualties, but we persevered. Eventually, the Egyptians surrendered.

After the battle at al-Fallujah, my orders sent me to another base, Bilu, near G'dara. From there, I went to Bayt Jibrin, where the Arabs ambushed and killed a group of about forty. The soldiers fighting for Israel's independence had been so badly butchered that they were unrecognizable. We honored them by burying them together in the military section of the cemetery in Rechovot. More death, more graves, but the fact that we were free and were fighting for the goal of a Jewish homeland provided some comfort and motivation.

We fought a fierce battle near Negba, and then we were sent to Be'er-Sheva, inhabited mostly by Bedouins, where we stayed in a fortress that also served as the police station.

Had there been a Jewish State during World War II, a safe haven where Jews would have been welcome, perhaps the Holocaust would never have happened. How different my own life would have been, and how different the course of history might have been.

We were young, but we did not fear death. We had seen it, smelled it, and felt it, like a blanket wrapped around our souls. We were a group of wild savages with no one in the world but each other and with nothing to lose. Our aggression and pent-up anger had created a dangerous and fearless group of fighters. At least we had begun the process of normalization before being sent off to fight in the War of Independence. Others were sent directly to the front line, straight from transport ships arriving from Europe.

I worked alongside the brigade chief, sending and receiving encoded messages until the summer of 1949. We used Morse Code at night and other secret codes utilizing Hebrew numbers and words, which we changed every few weeks to avoid detection.

Five of us from Santa Maria who stayed together throughout our journey from Italy to Palestine, and from the *kibbutz* to the Army, fought alongside one another in the War of Independence for the

State of Israel. It was also a time of confusion for me. Each day and each battle blended into the next. I was still processing the loss and despair from years in the camps, and still grieving the loss of my former life – my family, my friends, my town. It was difficult to process the immense losses the Jewish people as a whole had suffered that we continued to learn more about with each passing day; but, it was equally grueling for me to sort out my own personal catastrophe. I kept my feelings inside, choosing not to share them with my comrades, even though they too had experienced similar atrocities. We soldiered on, literally and metaphorically.

Our *kibbutz* faced a shortage of manpower, so as soon as we received our temporary discharge from the Army in the autumn, we returned to Sarid to assist however we could. We were discharged from service prior to the Armistice Agreements being signed between Israel and Lebanon, Israel and Egypt, Israel and Syria, and Israel and Transjordan. I knew little of the political situation, but I recognized that things had settled down and we no longer had to fight.

We soon heard about an alcohol spirits factory abandoned by its former Arab owners in Kfar Ata, so we left the *kibbutz* to stay in the abandoned building. The unfinished structure consisted of four walls and a roof with a sand floor and holes in the walls for windows. We hung blankets over the openings to keep out the cold, and we slept on the sand. It was possibly ten feet by ten feet, with no furniture, no running water, no kitchen, and no bathroom, but it was not the worst place we had ever lived, and we were grateful to have shelter, no matter how crude. I suppose we wanted our independence, and not to have to live by anyone else's rules. We were young and impetuous, and needed to keep moving forward, staying busy so that we could not dwell on our past.

Yosef Kalikwaser, a friend from Wierzbnik who had also survived the war, had made his way to Palestine and was also living in Kfar Ata. He heard that I was living in the abandoned spirits factory and came to visit me.

"How can you live like this?" he said, "Even animals do not live like this." He often invited me to his house to share a meal with him and his wife and to spend the night. His place was just a fraction more civilized than mine and perhaps not even as large, but he and his wife insisted that I visit. As there were no extra beds, I stayed on the floor, which was covered in wood, not sand as in my humble dwelling. Yosef, who was older than I and married, had a better sense of civility; I was doing the best I could, dealing with all the loss and damage to my life. I was struggling, but moving ahead. And I continued talking to myself, determined to press on.

Job opportunities were scarce, but some of my friends and I found work two days a week, performing manual labor for the government. We worked in a warehouse, unloading and carrying steel pipes from the ships at the Port of Haifa.

How glorious to be on this side of the port, and not seeing it from the Mediterranean, as I had from the deck of the Kaf Gimel.

We unloaded trucks, carried bricks, and transported cement in wheelbarrows. It was physically exhausting labor, but we worked without the constant dread of death, without the fear that comes from the randomness of cruelty meted out by our former Nazi captors. We worked hard, but we had enough to eat. We were tired, but we could rest without retribution. When we were thirsty, we could drink. We did not complain, for we were free men. We were doing our duty, helping the State of Israel construct the local Ministry of Labor building. We were proud veterans of Israel's War of Independence. We had achieved something. We had fought hard to ensure a strong, safe Jewish homeland.

I was never in a DP Camp, but I remained a displaced person, a young man without a home and without a family. Maybe some in DP camps had it easier. They had resources that we didn't have. I was drifting in chaos. I suffered terribly after the war, but it was a different suffering than when I was in the labor camps or concentration camps. I was now alone in the world, faced with adult decisions. Inside, I was hard-boiled and bitter. Before the age of sixteen years old, I knew how to steal, how to get on a train without paying, how to bury a corpse, and how to manipulate people to get what I needed. I am not proud of these things, but they helped me survive my captivity, and the early years of my liberation. I couldn't afford to misread people's intentions. If I did, like so many others I might end up dead like Yaakov Milman's children. Yaakov believed that the policeman, Tomczyk, would protect and hide his children, but Yaakov misjudged Tomczyk, and his children wound up dead. Even my parents may have misjudged the Polish family who was supposed to take Chaskel for safekeeping, for they too failed to live up to those expectations. There was always a risk when dealing with non-Jews or strangers, whether money was exchanged for a favor or not, but one often had to take a chance. I found it better to follow my instincts when attempting to read people.

By the age of fourteen, I had lost nearly my entire family, my friends, my home, my town, my community, and my faith in God. I had been a slave, had been deprived, and had been psychologically, emotionally, and physically tortured. I had almost starved to death, threatened with the gas chamber – twice – and threatened with a firing squad. I had seen and experienced things that no one, of any age, should. Now I had to build a life of purpose.

Winter was coming, and the rains began. We were constantly killing rats that were larger than the shoes we used to kill them. I was tiring of this appalling existence and needed to move on. I suggested that the five of us join the border police, but I was too short. My friend, Chaim Shier, was also too short, so he had a shoemaker build up a platform in his shoes to make him taller.

I was reminded of when Kiva and I were too short for selection and how we stood on pails to make ourselves appear taller. What had become of Kiva? He had provided me with support and companionship for so long, and now I had no idea whether he had even survived the death march or what had befallen him. I hoped for the best, but did not seek him out. I was busy tending to my immediate physical needs.

While we were in the midst of applying for the border police, I received correspondence from the International Red Cross with important news.

I had not searched any Red Cross lists. I had no energy for such pursuits, and I didn't hold out hope that I would find anyone alive who meant anything to me. But the Red Cross had received an inquiry about me. Had I survived the war and, if so, where was I living?

Who could be looking for me? A cousin? An old friend from Wierzbnik? Kiva?

It took a while for the Red Cross to locate me, as I had been using various names with a variety of different spellings. This was common among survivors. Some adopted more Hebrew sounding names; some took names of different branches of their own families. These assumed names made it difficult for the Red Cross or individuals to find surviving family members, but it gave some survivors a new identity. I opened the sealed envelope with the Red Cross logo on it. I took out the letter and slowly read the correspondence. My eyes panned over the letter as I read and then reread the inquiry, and let the implausible news sink in – *a miracle* – a miracle as great as my own survival from being sent to the gas chambers, not once but twice, a miracle as great as my survival of the death march and my survival of Mauthausen and Gunskirchen, or even my survival having been a soldier fighting for Israel's independence. The Red Cross inquiry had come from Canada, from my mother, who had also miraculously survived. My mother was alive!

Some survivors had told my mother not to look for me – that I had been killed in Birkenau. Some had apparently heard that I had been sent to the quarantine barracks and then to the gas chambers, but obviously they were unaware of how, on Rosh Hashanah, I ran and hid myself in the little oven in the barrack, or how, on Yom Kippur, my uncle bribed the *kapo* and I was saved yet again. Some survivors had given my mother false information, but others may have heard rumors of my survival, or were just giving her hope to keep searching for me.

I learned from my mother's correspondence that after the war ended, my mother encountered a family friend from Wierzbnik, Alter Weisbloom. He had lost his wife and children in the war. My mother had also heard that my father died in the camps, and she knew about my brother, her parents and other family lost in Treblinka. Poles warned Alter Weisbloom and my mother against remaining in Wierzbnik, so instead they traveled to Lodz, a larger, more cosmopolitan city. But anti-Semitism persisted and indignities against Jews continued although the war was over.

It was typical of Holocaust survivors to bury the past and move on as quickly as possible after the war. Survivors clung to one another, married, and created new families. In many cases, survivors never spoke of former spouses or of children lost in the war. It was too painful. This was true for both my mother and Alter Weisbloom, who had both suffered terrible losses: parents, spouses, children, and others. My mother and Alter Weisbloom held fast to one another and soon married. It gave my mother some stability, some identity. It gave them both companionship and the love they each desperately needed. They stayed in Lodz for a short while before heading to Munich, where they remained until 1948, when they obtained their papers to emigrate to Canada. Surprisingly, Jews had an easier time in Germany after the war, as it was controlled by the United States and its allies, as opposed to Poland, which had fallen to the Communists, the eastern side of the Iron Curtain.

Although many Nazis slipped back into German society, escaping any penalty for their involvement in persecution of Jews, Gypsies, Catholics, and others, some ordinary Germans realized the magnitude of the Nazi atrocities and sought to make amends. Some Nazis were tried for their crimes, and reparations to victims of their crimes were beginning to be formulated and put into place.

Relatives of my mother in Toronto encouraged her to search

for me, despite rumors of my death. They assisted her in contacting the Red Cross in Canada. By some miracle, the Red Cross found me through the many lists and registries that documented survivors of the war. They gave my mother the address for *Kibbutz* Sarid. I was shocked to receive her correspondence and to learn that she too had survived. I genuinely did not believe that my mother, given her age and all that she had suffered, could possibly have made it through the death march, but here was the proof that she was alive and well, living in Toronto, Canada, and writing to me, a letter in my mother's own handwriting. There was no question that I would go to Canada, that I was compelled to go, even though I had learned Hebrew, fought for the establishment of the State of Israel, and had an unbreakable bond with the boys from whom I'd been inseparable since Santa Maria. Nothing could take precedence or priority over the fact that a member of my family, a blood relative, especially my beloved mother, had indeed survived.

My mother and I corresponded for several months. She would send mail to my cousin's house in Haifa, at Rechov Zvulun Street, 5. With each letter, she sent two dollars. My cousin, Arieh, would exchange the dollars into shekels, so I would have a little extra to live on. Through our correspondence, I learned that my mother had survived Auschwitz and was sent on the death march.

How did my mother survive?

After the second day of the death march, she was left for dead in a ditch along the side of the road in the freezing Polish winter.

Perhaps we were not far from one another when each of our bodies failed to cooperate and our strength was lost, when we both gave up our efforts to take another step forward. Perhaps we were not far from one another when we each collapsed in the snow.

While the Germans transported me to Mauthausen, the advancing Russian troops soon found my mother, and took her to a hospital where she was treated and allowed to recuperate. When the doctors released her from the hospital, against all warnings, my mother remained in Poland to seek family survivors.

Lodz became a gathering place for Jewish survivors to reconnect, to congregate, and to gather information. There, my mother was astounded to find her sister. The two returned to Wierzbnik together, and my mother was able to retrieve photos and some documents she had entrusted to our Polish friends, the Spytkowskis, during the ghetto period, including the deed to our house and the warehouse. For a pittance, my mother exchanged the deed to our house – the house that my grandfather had built, and where I had wonderful memories of Chaskel, and where I spent holidays with family. The Poles, who had essentially stolen our home and moved in while we were imprisoned, gave my mother the equivalent of a mere $500. She sold the warehouse for about $1,000. These sums were a token, a fraction of the real value of the land, the building, and the efforts of my grandparents and parents in constructing them. But my mother was fortunate to have retrieved anything at all. She was also lucky to get out of Wierzbnik alive. Others who returned were not so fortunate.

Poles treated Jews returning to Wierzbnik with disdain, even killing them with impunity, owing to their deep-seated anti-Semitism and greed. They did not want to relinquish whatever property they had stolen from their former neighbors. My mother learned that on June 8, 1945, two women and two children were murdered after returning to Wierzbnik to look for missing friends and relatives. It was a lawless time; there were no consequences for a Pole killing a Jew.

I received my permanent discharge papers from the Army on May 22, 1949, and obtained a visa to enter Canada. There was no Canadian embassy in Israel at the time, so I had to get a visa from the British Embassy, representing Canada through the Commonwealth. I hitchhiked to the embassy in Tel Aviv, but by the time I got my permit to leave the Army, my visa had expired, so I had to return to the embassy. Nothing was easy within the bureaucracy of this new country, but I was grateful for my freedom, and grateful that I had contributed to the birth of the State of Israel.

While my four friends joined the border police, I prepared for the long trip to my new home of Canada. I packed a small bag with just a pair of shoes, shorts, and not much else. I didn't even have a pair of trousers. A friend from Wierzbnik, Lis Shuali, then known by his adopted Hebrew name, Eliezer, brought me two shirts for my journey to Canada. My mother sent me a suit that my friend, Yosef Kalikwaser, a tailor, altered for me. I also possessed the plane ticket my mother had provided.

In the early morning of December 1, 1949, my cousin, Arieh, who used to visit me at *Atlit,* brought me to the airport at Lod, now known as Ben Gurion Airport. He handed me ten U.S. dollars. I boarded the small British Airways propeller plane that carried perhaps twelve passengers. I had never been on an airplane. I was nervous, but I was on my way to Canada to join my remaining family. It was a noisy and bumpy flight to Rome, where we landed to refuel. Unlike the first time I arrived in Italy, hidden away by the Jewish Brigade, I now entered legally. From Rome, we continued westward to London. At this time, I spoke Yiddish, Polish, German, Hebrew, and some Italian, but not a word of English. A man sitting next to me helped me fill out the immigration forms.

I spent the night at a London hotel, but because I did not speak English, I did not know how to order anything to eat. I couldn't make out any of the English signs on the streets or in the hotel. I rode the hotel elevator up and down a few times, not knowing what to do or where to go. Finally, I gestured to the hotel staff, indicating that I was hungry. They pointed the way to the restaurant where I enjoyed a simple meal. Everything was foreign to me.

The next day, I boarded a British Airways plane bound for Canada. This was a larger propeller plane designed for crossing the Atlantic Ocean.

What would mother look like after five years of being separated? Would she have aged from the stress of the war and all her incredible losses? What would it be like now that she was married to Alter Weisbloom and not to my father? Would my broken heart be open for fresh possibilities in my new life in Canada?

As the airplane ascended, I watched the lush green English countryside fade from view and wondered where life would take me now. As it turned out, my return to London would come unwelcomely soon.

Several hours into the bumpy flight, the stewardess notified the passengers that as a result of inclement weather, the pilot was returning to London. I didn't understand English, but fellow passengers attempted to explain why the plane was veering back. I understood that we would not reach Canada that day; the anticipation of reuniting with my mother was extinguished. In London, I returned to the same hotel. Once again, I was all alone in this strange country, and even though I looked forward to the reunion with my mother, I felt lonely. As always, I talked to myself, urging myself onward.

The following day, I boarded the same noisy propeller plane, and took a deep breath. Once again, we took off and headed toward Canada: the New World, North America, the land where my mother's father did not dare to go, for it was *"not kosher enough, not holy enough."* Not that Europe had welcomed his religious customs and traditions. Rather, Europe had turned against his religion, massacred it, decimated it, and buried it in a continent-wide grave. I wondered what awaited me now.

Will I adjust? Will I find others whom I know from Poland or the camps? Will I find a job without a formal education, or a trade, or the ability to speak English?

Once again, several hours into our flight, the stewardess informed us that because of inclement weather, the pilot was returning the plane to England.

Five years had passed since the last time I saw my mother, when the men and women were boarded onto trains from Starachowice, headed for Auschwitz. It was like another lifetime. So much had happened between that last goodbye and now. So much that we could never share with one another openly, but that we each knew. Even in my effort to rejoin my mother in Canada, these fits and starts were a reminder of the difficult roads we had each traveled – across continents and oceans and the ever-difficult journey that still had yet to unfold.

By the following day, I was used to the routine. I took my seat on the propeller plane and fitted the buckle into the strap. And once again, we rolled down the runway and lifted off. Only this time, we were truly on our way. I had many hours to think. I can't even remember what language I was thinking in. Hebrew? Yiddish? But I thought about everything I had learned and experienced in my short life. All those lessons had educated and informed me. I was the quintessential archetype of 20th century Eastern European Jewry. I was a Holocaust survivor, a *kibbutznik, and* a veteran of Israel's War of Independence. I had seen it all.

During the transatlantic flight, I thought about why there is so much hatred of the Jewish people. I wonder if it was because certain sects of Jews, such as the Hasidim, are a minority with a highly identifiable appearance, with their long black coats and tall black hats, long beards, and *payos*, and for their habit of separating themselves from society rather than integrating into their host country. Jews were not understood, and history has shown again and again that men fear, and try to control, that which they do not understand. Jews have always made it a point to remember past perpetrators of crimes against them, from the Pharaohs of Egypt, to Haman of Persia, to Queen Isabella and King Ferdinand of Spain, and every other anti-Semitic leader who sought to enslave, convert, or expel the Jews. Others likely resent the Jews for their adherence to certain customs and traditions. Whether this animosity derives from unfounded xenophobia, or from plain jealousy, I do not know. I do believe that even though some Jews have assimilated, all Jews are simply grouped together as one discernible group in other people's eyes, but it is difficult for me to understand the targeting of an entire people.

I wondered why more people did not flee Europe before the

Holocaust began, but it was almost impossible to imagine that an effort to exterminate an entire culture would ensue. Those Jews who stayed, apart from those too old, too young, or too infirm to leave, deluded themselves into believing that human beings would behave in a civilized manner. Unfortunately, the unique case of the Holocaust illustrates that even good and decent people are capable of the most horrific acts.

As we advanced toward Canada, "The New World," *my* new world, I considered how far I'd come. I thought about coming out of the abyss that had been my life during the war years, and I hoped for a happier future. There is no benefit to looking at other's good fortune and feeling a sense of jealousy. There will always be some with more or less, whether it be luck, or good fortune, but I realized that nothing good comes from coveting another's good fortune. All the loss and deprivation I had experienced taught me to be present in the moment, to be fully aware, to follow my instinct, my gut. I learned to swallow my pain, and somehow found a way to smile again.

While I might have lost my faith in God, I remained Jewish. I would celebrate Jewish holidays, and carry on Jewish traditions. I knew that one day I would raise a Jewish family, teaching my children the history of our people and passing on the customs I held in my heart. I did not consider myself a religious person, but a certain way of life was instilled in me, and I owed it to the memories of my grandparents and my father to keep the lamp of Judaism lit for future generations. Jewish continuity.

I stared at the bluish-green tattoo etched on my arm: A18805. It would always be there as a reminder. I was inescapably linked to the war, to the Holocaust. I had been a prisoner, punished without having committed any crime, but I knew that I was more than just a number, and even though I could not escape my past, I did not want that tattoo to define me either. I needed to keep moving forward so it would not consume me like the flames that engulfed the dead bodies in the crematoria. I survived by chance, by a sequence of events that guarded me, protected me, and saved me from death over and over. It was *b'shert,* but it was not without its downside. During the war I did not ask, *"Why me?"* I simply pushed onward with an attitude of *"What now? What can I do right now in this moment to remain alive?"* After the war, however, and after I was out of harm's immediate path, the pain and survivor guilt set in.

Why him and not me? Why me and not him? Why?

And then there were the questions of justice and revenge, and what to do with the anger that I lugged around. I could not hold children of the Nazis accountable, or children of collaborators: Poles, Ukrainians. Each person is responsible for his or her own actions, but I could not absolve those who overtly took steps to turn in Jews, knowing that the fate of those Jews would be certain death. I did not feel hatred or anger toward all Germans or all Poles, for some had shown kindness, or took risks to help us at their own peril. I was determined not to psychologically remain in the camps. I had no time for revenge; I only had time to get on with my life. I was a born optimist, and throughout the war I didn't believe in dying, only struggling to live day by day. Although I could not be sure of my eventual survival, I was always hoping I would make it. I told myself that all the bad things were behind me, and that things would only get better. I had survived the impossible, and had no parental guidance after the war. I was trying to make adult decisions, with only a second grade education, and the trauma that had been my adolescence. I realized the real-life instruction I learned was essential in helping me land on my feet at each and every turn along the way.

The plane touched down in Newfoundland, Canada, where we refueled, before landing next in Montreal. During our flight and during the layover in Montreal, a gentleman on the plane kept asking, *"Whiskey? Whiskey?"* and gesturing as if he were taking a drink. My lack of English made me feel very vulnerable, but whiskey did much to settle my nerves and warm me from the inside. It numbed the pain. Around midnight on December 4th, the plane landed in Toronto.

My mother's cousin brought her and her friend, Rose Milman, to the airport to greet me. My mother and I had last seen each other in Tartak, the woodworking factory in Poland. So many unthinkable, unspeakable things had happened to both of us since, and we could not talk about any of it. We lacked the vocabulary, and the will, to open the floodgates of what had transpired since leaving the woodworking factory in our lost and lifeless town. We could not let the past into our present, or it would consume us. It was another lifetime for us, and it was enough that we were just alive and in each other's presence.

At first, I didn't feel much when I saw her. I recognized my mother, of course, but she had aged beyond her years, and I had already learned to live with the loss of my family. I had swallowed the thought of them and pushed their memories to the deep recesses of my mind. Now, my mother stood before me, as if an apparition. It was difficult for my eyes to focus on what I was really seeing. I had already processed the loss, already mourned the deaths of both my parents and my brother, and now it was tough to undo that work and allow myself to feel. Now I could lose her a second time. It was probably equally difficult for my mother when she first laid eyes on me too. I was now 19, practically a man. She had seen me last when I was a mere boy, skinny and scared, doing whatever I could to remain useful in Tartak. Men and women were separated on the trains to Auschwitz-Birkenau, and I had not seen my mother nor heard news of her once we left Starachowice.

Since then I had survived the worst of the war, and created a new life for myself in Israel. I had a band of brothers whom I'd first met in Italy. They were my support system from then on, and were by my side as we fought for Israel's independence, and now I was in a strange country, with another new language yet to learn, and a mother I no longer knew, a mother who had moved on with her life and remarried. There was a silence between us that we dared not address. It was not my place to ask, and my mother did not offer. As any son, I had mixed emotions about my mother moving on, but I knew that was the way of the world, that was life. Some things were beyond our control. Some things we just did not question. I had to accept it and move on with my own life. And, as awkward as our initial reunion felt to me, I was overcome with a most powerful emotion.

GRATITUDE

I WAS GRATEFUL for my mother's presence, her survival, and my own. I felt fortunate to have had the strength to talk myself through all the tough times I'd been through, to know myself, and to know the core of my very being. I was determined not only to survive, but to thrive in spite of it all. I felt keenly aware of the miracle of the future that lay before me as I remembered the *Torah's* commandment: Choose Life. This was forefront in my mind; and through a series of miracles, big and small, I survived the atrocities of the Holocaust.

Indeed, I chose life. And life, without a doubt, has also chosen me.

AFTERWORD

THE TRIAL OF WALTHER BECKER
– YET ANOTHER INJUSTICE

WALTHER BECKER ESCAPED from Poland in January 1945, and like so many former Nazis and Nazi sympathizers, he rejoined civil society without any consequence for his part in the enslavement, torture, and death of many innocents.

Becker returned to Hamburg, Germany, where they welcomed him back on the police force. During this post-war period, some tried to hold Nazi perpetrators accountable, and the British temporarily suspended Becker from his job because of questions surrounding his wartime activities. Becker was reinstated to his police position in 1947. German authorities continued to investigate his wartime activities, and in 1951, he was again temporarily suspended from the police force – with pay. When he retired in 1957, he did so with a complete pension.

In 1961, survivors came forward to give testimony about Becker's wartime activities. This time an arrest warrant was issued, but the order was lifted on the condition that Becker report to authorities at least three times per week. In 1970, the German consulate in Toronto, where a number of former Wierzbnikers had relocated after the war, informed us that Walther Becker was finally going to be tried in Germany for crimes committed on the day of the liquidation of the ghetto, but not for any other crimes he committed during his five-year tenure as the security police branch officer in Starachowice.

I was eager to volunteer to testify against Becker and relate what I knew from the day of the *Aktia,* including my personal observation of Becker ordering people into groups going to the work camp, or instead to the trains headed for Treblinka. I observed him when I presented him with my work card, which he promptly tore up, sending me back to the group destined for the trains. I saw him again days later in Tartak, when he questioned my age. I personally witnessed Becker beating people, giving orders, threatening people with his revolver, and I saw him at the market square the day of the hanging of the Poles, but I did not witness him shoot anyone. But I know what I saw with my own eyes on the day of the liquidation – that he was in charge and directing the operation, determining which poor souls would be sent directly to the Treblinka death camp. However, I was deemed to have been too young at the time to be considered a credible witness.

Before the trial, I spoke to many survivors about their recollections of Becker, and I suspect I remembered more details about him than did many of the older workers. Even my mother and stepfather agreed to testify. My mother must have been nervous about returning to Germany, but I knew that she and the others felt a strong sense of obligation on behalf of all those who did not survive. The trial represented a chance to bring out the truth, punish some of those responsible, and achieve some sliver of justice. My mother commented that it was not as difficult to face Becker in court because he was no longer wearing his uniform.

Walther Becker was a veteran of World War I. He joined the German Socialist Party in 1930, was temporarily suspended from his work as a police officer, but was reinstated in 1933. In 1937 he joined the Nazi party. He applied for membership in the *Schutzstaffel (SS),* but his application was never approved. In 1940 he was sent to Starachowice. From 1941 to 1945, he was in charge of the branch office of the Security Police in the region.

The trial began in August, 1971 and lasted seven months. There were numerous court sessions during which nearly one hundred witnesses, both Jewish and German, testified, and many depositions were read into evidence. It was a *Schwurgericht* trial, a hybrid form of a bench trial and a jury trial together, to be juried by a nine-judge panel.

On February 8, 1972, the verdict was handed down. Not only did Becker get away with murder, but he was compensated for the three days when he was held in police custody, and he was allowed to keep his police pension. The trial was an absolute travesty of justice, exemplifying how the Nazi party elite had returned to society without being held accountable for their actions.

The court accepted that Becker was not in charge of overseeing Jewish affairs in Starachowice, that he did not know about the deportation of the Jews, that he did not participate in the roundup and selection of the Jews on the day of the *Aktia*, and that he did not know that the Jews were to be killed at Treblinka. The court turned the system of eyewitness testimony on its head by declaring that the Jewish eye witnesses' testimony was unreliable because they were not "disinterested" or "detached." The court also took the position that because of the time that had elapsed between the events about which they were testifying and the actual trial, that the eyewitness testimony was untrustworthy. The court summarily dismissed much of the witnesses' testimony as inconsistent or unreliable if they testified with more details than they had given when originally questioned during previous interviews, if they had not given a previous deposition, or if the witness gave a deposition, but then did not appear in court. The court further dismissed any testimony if the witness was too young at the time of the liquidation (like me), or was too old at the time of the trial. The court even dismissed those who showed emotion while testifying. In so doing, the court eliminated the eyewitness accounts of virtually all who provided damning testimony against Becker.

Christopher Browning, a history professor at the University of

North Carolina at Chapel Hill, and who has written several books on the Holocaust, including *Remembering Survival*, which tells the story of Wierzbnik and the slave labor camps of Starachowice, reviewed original materials and primary sources from the Becker trial. Browning notes that the German criminal code in place at the time of the post-war trials was inadequate to successfully prosecute war criminals, and that the German court system itself was infiltrated by judges and lawyers who were former Nazis who sympathized with the defendants. The judge in the Becker trial was Wolf-Dietrich Ehrhardt. He became a lawyer before the war, and had fought in the German army, rising to the rank of first lieutenant by its end. After the war, he became a judge. Browning's research revealed that Ehrhardt applied to become a member of the SS but was denied when his background check revealed that he had some non-Aryan ancestors. Therefore, he could not prove that he had five generations of racial purity, as required for membership into the SS. Who knows why a man who was rejected from the SS because of his non-Aryan blood would still want to assist criminals such as Becker, but that is the sad truth of the complexity of the war and of the Holocaust. Crimes were committed, and most of those responsible were never held accountable for those crimes. Although Becker was never punished for his crimes, the truth of who he was, and what he did, has been told.

Martin, Chaskel and Chaja
Baranek, Wierzbnik, Poland

Martin Baranek,
Rabka, Poland,1939

Martin Baranek,
Rabka, Poland 1939

Modena, Italy, Martin Baranek seated in middle, 1945

*Zvi Unger, Max Naiman, Martin
Baranek Modena, Italy, 1945*

*Zvi Unger, Max Naiman, Martin Baranek, Arie
Leib Rosenberg, Modena, Italy 1945*

*Geulim, Santa Maria al Bagno, Italy, 1945, Martin
Baranek is seated in the first row, third from the right*

Martin Baranek at Kibbutz Sarid, Palestine

Army base, Israel 1948

WHAT BECAME OF...

Howard Chandler

Howard and I knew each other from Wierzbnik, and attended *Cheder* together. He was two years ahead of me in school. His house fronted the town square of Wierzbnik. Howard had a work permit for one of the labor camps in Starachowice. We were transported together to Auschwitz with the rest of the prisoners from the Starachowice camps. During the death march, Howard wound up on a train to Buchenwald, from which he was later liberated. Howard first went to England, before emigrating to Canada. Whenever a Wierzbniker arrived in Toronto, the entire community came out to greet that person. That is how Howard and I were reunited. Howard has participated in the March of the Living several times, and Education Without Borders, which takes students to Poland to learn firsthand about the Holocaust. We often reminisce about our town and those who were lost. Howard and his wife Elsa split their time between Toronto and Miami.

Kiva Kadysiewicz

After we were separated on the death march, Kiva was sent to Bergen Belsen from where he was liberated. He later emigrated to Canada. In the late 1950s he married and had two daughters and a son. Although Kiva physically left the camps, the camps never left Kiva psychologically and emotionally, and he spent the rest of his life struggling to overcome his past. Kiva passed away in Toronto in 2013.

Nora Markowic

After the war, my aunt Sara went to the convent where the Poles had abandoned my cousin Nora. Sara learned that the convent had transferred Nora to a convent in France. The nuns at the convent refused to turn over her daughter, but my aunt would not be deterred. A Jewish organization called BRAICHA, which helped reclaim Jewish kids who hid during the war, helped Sara smuggle Nora from France to Germany, and with the help of relatives, they emigrated to Canada. Soon after arriving in Canada, Nora contracted polio, which left her debilitated. After several surgeries, she was able to walk with a limp. Nora married and had two daughters. She passed away in 2013.

Moishe Szpagat

My cousin Moishe was liberated from Mauthausen. After the war he returned to Poland and was soon married. Shortly afterward, he and his wife moved to Belgium, where his wife had family. They emigrated to Canada in 1951. He and his wife had two children. His wife passed away in 2016. Six weeks later, his eldest son passed away. He currently resides in Toronto.

Zvi Unger

After we separated in Italy, Zvi returned to Germany to search for his sister. He found her in a DP camp. She went to Palestine on an illegal ship, but she passed away in Cyprus. Zvi emigrated to Israel in 1948. While serving in the Army, he lost his right hand. After The War of Independence, the government assisted him in opening a perfume store in Natanya. He married and had one son, Yossi, who still resides in Israel. Zvi passed away in Israel in 2009.

A NEW LIFE IN CANADA

WHEN MARTIN FIRST arrived in Canada, he lived in a Yiddish-speaking immigrant community near Toronto's Bathurst Street, and worked in a clothing factory with other newly arrived immigrants, where he earned $20 per week. After several years, he worked his way up to $78 per week, but he knew that to become the master of his own destiny, he would have to become his own boss. Martin worked hard, learned English, obtained a bank loan, and, like his mother back in Wierzbnik, started a grocery store. He and his future business partner, Jack Bursztain, also a Holocaust survivor, joined the Independent Grocers Alliance and expanded from one store to four. They sold the business in 2001.

Martin married Betty Eidelman on October 11, 1953. Betty and her parents had survived the war in Siberia. Like Martin, they had emigrated from Europe to Palestine before settling in Canada.

Martin seldom spoke about the war or his experiences in any great detail until his grandson began questioning him about it for a school project. Since then, he has become actively involved in the March of the Living. Martin has traveled to Poland and Israel at least two dozen times with students and adults, teaching them about the Holocaust from his personal experience, in the places where the atrocities actually occurred.

At a Holocaust Remembrance Day Ceremony, the Premier of

Ontario, in conjunction with the Canadian Society for Yad Vashem, recognized Martin as an honoree at the 2013 Queen's Park Tribute.

Martin and Betty raised three sons and one daughter, and have nine grandchildren. Tragically, their eldest son, Morry, passed away from cancer in 2001. Their reward in life has been to see all of their children become university-educated, and they enjoy knowing that their grandchildren will continue the family's commitment to Jewish continuity, higher education and personal responsibility.

Now retired, Martin and Betty divide their time between Toronto and Miami.

GLOSSARY

Aktzia: Typically used to describe the liquidation of a town or ghetto; the rounding up of Jews to be sent either to work camps, concentration camps, or death camps; or to be murdered and buried in mass graves

Anti-Semitism: Hatred toward Jews; hostility toward or discrimination against Jews as a religious, ethnic, or racial group

Appel: A roll call

Ashkenazi: A member of one of the two great divisions of Jews comprising the eastern European Yiddish-speaking Jews; compared to Sephardim, members of the occidental branch of European Jews settling in Spain and Portugal and later in the Balkans, the Levant, England, the Netherlands, and the Americas

Bet Midrash: Literally "House of Learning" refers to a Jewish study hall located in a synagogue, yeshiva, kollel or other building

Bris/Brit: The Jewish rite or ceremony of male circumcision, usually performed on the eighth day of life

B'shert: Destined; also refers to one's destined mate or spouse

Challah: Braided egg bread for celebrations including Shabbat and holidays

Chametz: Leavened products forbidden on Pesach

Chanukah: Winter holiday commemorating the Maccabees battle in which they defeated the Syrian Hellenists; also referred to as the Festival of Lights.

Cheder: Religious lesson, also refers to the place where religious lessons are held as in a school or synagogue

Cheshvan: 2nd Jewish month on the Hebrew calendar, which corresponds to the secular calendar during the months of October - November

Chevra Kadisha: Holy association; burial society

Chuppah: Traditional wedding canopy

Chutzpah: Sass, moxie, nerve, gall

Gminna: Jewish leadership within the ghettos

Hagaddah: Pesach guidebook, used during Seder

Haganah: Literally translated from Hebrew as "defence," the Jewish paramilitary organization operating in Palestine while still under British rule. The Haganah became the foundation of Israel's current military, the Israel Defense Forces ("IDF")

Hamantashen: Purim cookies filled with fruit or poppy seeds

Hassidic: Member of a sect founded in Poland in the 18th century by Baal Shem-Tov and characterized by its emphasis on mysticism, prayer, ritual strictness, religious zeal, and joy

Jewish ghetto: Third Reich created Jewish ghetto-system for the purpose of persecution, terror, and exploitation of Jews, mostly in Eastern Europe, established at least 1,000 ghettos in German-occupied and annexed Poland and Soviet Union

Jude: Jew

Judenrat: Council of ghetto Jews charged with picking Jews to give to Nazis for delivery to concentration/death camps

Kaddish: Mourner's prayer

Kosher: Food that is permissible to eat under Jewish law

Krajowa Army: (AK, the Home Army) was the dominant Polish resistance movement in World War II German-occupied Poland, formed in February 1942 from the Zwiazek Walki Zbroinei (Armed Resistance); allegiance to the Polish Government-in-exile, and constituted the armed wing of what became known as the "Polish Underground State"

Kristallnacht: "Night of Broken Glass," Nazi pogrom on November 9 -10, 1938; the worst pogrom ever, marking beginning of the Holocaust

Ludowa: Armia Ludowa (AL, the *People's Army*) was a communist partisan force set up by the communist Polish Workers' Party (*PPR*) during World War II, formed by the Polish State National Council on January 1, 1944 to fight against Nazi Germans in occupied Poland, support the Soviet military against the German forces and to aid in the creation of a pro-Soviet Union communist government in Poland, one of the military resistance organizations that refused to join the structures of the "Polish Underground State" or its military arm, the Home Army (AK)

Melamed: A religious teacher who is a non-rabbi

Mikve: a ritual bath to which Orthodox Jews are traditionally required to go on certain occasions to cleanse and purify themselves

Mitzvah: Religious commandment; a good deed

Payos: Long sideburns worn by Chasidim

Pesach: Spring holiday also known as Passover, commemorating the exodus of the Hebrew slaves from Egypt

Purim: Spring holiday (on the 14th or 15th day of Adar) to commemorate the defeat of Haman's plot to massacre the Jews as recorded in the book of Esther

Rabbi: A Jewish scholar or teacher, especially one who studies or teaches Jewish law, a person appointed as a Jewish religious leader

Revizia: Typically, an unannounced search of one's home by German soldiers who might confiscate any personal belongings or make any arrests

Rosh Hashanah: Fall holiday "Head of the year," Jewish New Year

Rynek: A marketplace or market square in Polish towns and cities established in the Middle Ages

Schlepper: One who carries, drags, lugs; also to drag one's feet; travel a great distance

Schutzstaffel: An elite military unit of the Nazi party that served as Hitler's bodyguards and as a special police force

Seder: Pesach ceremonial meal

Shabbat: Sabbath, observed from sunset on Friday evening until sunset on Saturday; Jewish day of rest

Shema: Jewish confession of faith made up of Deuteronomy 6:4–9 and 11:13–21 and Numbers 15:37–41

Shidach: Match; Jewish arranged marriage

Shiva: Period of mourning observed for seven days following a family member's funeral

Shlacha mones: To send presents; to bring sweets from one house to another for friends and family, especially on Purim

Shoah: Literally destruction; The Holocaust

Shomrim: Guards, Jewish custom of watching over a dead body before burial; watchers are known as *shomrim*

Shtetl: Eastern European Jewish village

Shtiebel: A place used for communal Jewish prayer. In contrast to a formal synagogue, a **shtiebel** is far smaller and approached more casually. It is typically as small as a room in a private home or a place of business that is set aside for the express purpose of prayer, or it may be as large as a small-sized synagogue. It may or may not offer the communal services of a synagogue.

SS Untersturmfuhrer: A paramilitary rank of the German *Schutzstaffel* (SS) first created in July 1934. The rank of *Untersturmführer* was senior to *Hauptscharführer* (or *Sturmscharführer* in the *Waffen-SS*) and junior to the rank of *Obersturmführer*.

Sukkot: Fall harvest festival holiday literally Feast of Booths, or Feast of Tabernacles, or Feast of the Ingathering, celebrated on the 15th day of the month of Tishrei on the Hebrew calendar corresponding to the secular months of September and October

Taharah: Jewish religious ceremony of washing a corpse before burial

Third Reich: The name given by the Nazis to their government in Germany; *Reich* is German for "empire." Adolf Hitler, their leader, believed that he was creating a third German empire, a successor to the Holy Roman Empire and the German empire formed by Chancellor Bismarck in the nineteenth century.

Torah, Sefer Torah: Scroll containing the Jewish law of God as revealed to Moses and recorded in the first five books of the Hebrew scriptures (the Pentateuch)

Treiger: carrier

Yeshiva: School for Talmudic study; an Orthodox Jewish rabbinical seminary; a Jewish day school providing secular and religious instruction

Yiddish: A language used by Jews in central and eastern Europe before the Holocaust. It was originally a German dialect with words from Hebrew and several modern languages

Yom Kippur: Jewish holiday observed with fasting and prayer on the 10th day of Tishri on the Hebrew calendar in accordance with the rites described in Leviticus 16 —called also *Day of Atonement*, observed during the secular months of September or October during which Jewish people do not eat or drink anything and pray to ask for forgiveness for mistakes made during the year

Yom Tov: Literally good day; holiday

Zayde: grandfather

Zloty: Basic monetary unit of Poland

CPSIA information can be obtained
at www.ICGtesting.com
Printed in the USA
LVHW032137280319
612255LV00001B/1/P